Emotions are Messages

Achieve Self-Mastery
by Learning to Work Safely with Your Anger, Sadness,
Worry and residues of Trauma.

Armand Kruger

Cover Illustration: Independent
Please note that all efforts have been made to contact the relevant parties regarding any possible infringement of copyright. Should you have any information regarding, please do not hesitate to contact us.

For permission requests, please contact the author at the contact details below:
armand@peakperformer.co.za

Web address: www.peakperformer.co.za

Emotions are Messages ISBN 978-0-620-78996-7 (printed book)
Emotions are Messages ISBN 78-0-620-78950-9 (e-book)

First Edition 2018

CONTENTS

Endorsements

"At the core of most of the destructive emotions, lies the emotion of fear in all its configurations. It is fear which perpetuates the destructive emotions in the individual, between individuals and in the environment at large. In this context, the concepts and applications proposed in this book by Armand Kruger become critical requirements for transcending the destructive emotions and arriving at a far more productive and gratifying space. Armand has recognised the fundamental problem and has proposed the solution – to use reasoning to unpack and reconfigure these emotions and establish a more sustaining state of mind."
Dr. Ian Weinberg
Author, Neuro-Surgeon

"The author takes you by the hand and carefully leads you to hitherto unknown corners of your psyche. You are reading your first steps to self-mastering! I hope you are courageous enough to continue and albeit fearful at times, know that you have stepped on to a wonderful dance floor!"
Susan van Hemert
NLP Advanced Practioner, Counsellor

"Once you have read the first chapter you will not want to put the book down. Armand brings clarity to the distinction between emotions and feelings and moves to a meta-position where emotions are to be understood as messages. How we portray these messages to others or respond to other peoples' messages is the key to dancing through the good life in a responsible, authentic and fulfilling way. Learning the dance is made easy by the way in which Armand brilliantly brings theory to practice."
Dr. Rod Waddington
HR Manager, Vusilela College

"If you are serious about knowing why emotions influence your daily life and want to take charge and pursue permanent change, this is the book to take up and read. In this book, Armand was able to share his lifelong experience and wisdom, not only from an academic perspective, but also in a practical way. This is a book that unlocks a treasure of interventions, for both the novice and the seasoned NLP-practitioner/psychologist."
Dr. Saneth Dreyer
Author, Psychologist in Private Practice

"Emotions are messages. The title immediately captured my attention. Messages of what? From whom? To whom? These questions and many more are being answered in this well-researched book. This book is an example of experiential wisdom, a knowledge gained from living it."
Hilda Kriel
Deputy Director: Department of Library Services

"Emotions are what makes us human. We see and feel the world of our reality through the eyes of emotions. Too much or too little emotion is detrimental to anyone. So where do we find the balance in our emotional life? The starting point is from within – start with the self; learn to unlearn the old pathways in your brain. This book gives you a clear starting point with guided questions to this vital internal journey."
Dr. Paul Erasmus
Cardiothoracic Surgeon

PREFACE

If a preface is the place for an author's confession, then I have two confessions to make.

Firstly, there was a time when I trusted my emotions. Then I learned some very painful and expensive lessons about not trusting my emotions. While doing therapy with people who asked for help with emotional issues, I frequently found myself pretending to know things about emotions that I was actually still asking myself. I stopped being a therapist. I met Steve and Connirae Andreas and, through them, qualified as a practitioner of Neuro-Linguistic-Programming. I felt like I had arrived! NLP was my home. I finally had some answers. The book was due.

Secondly, this book has been in the making for more than 20 years, but is still as valid as the day when I sat down with the intention of writing it so many years ago. Even though some fascinating research and ideas about emotions abound these days, not much additional and reliable information about "how to" live with emotions has appeared since I started to study the subject. As much as I tried to help other people live meaningfully with their emotions, I also wanted to understand my own. And it is a fascinating subject. Not only are emotions an ever-present aspect of our daily lives, but the same emotions can also have different meanings or messages in different situations. If we can understand it better, we can enrich our lives so much more. As Roger Fischer and Daniel Shapiro write in their book, Building Agreement – Using Emotions as you Negotiate: "We cannot stop having emotions any more than we can stop having thoughts. The challenge is learning to stimulate helpful emotions in those with whom we negotiate – and in ourselves."

There is an impressive the range of feel-good emotions, from merely helpful emotions to the ultimate caring of love; from sweetly smiling contentment through to the uncontainable shout-out-load exuberantly happy emotions. As an international NLP (Neuro-Linguistic Programming) trainer, my starting point for understanding the emotions was process: more the "how" than the "what" of emotions. This, to me, was more than a curiosity. I wanted to understand how you can come to grips with this "thinking with your heart". I wanted to know the "how" from a lived point of view. I wanted to be able to describe and name the common denominators of emotions. I wanted to understand the emotional wisdom I noticed in some people and how they were the richer for it.

The wisdom gained from understanding our emotions not only allows us to be beautiful people, but it opens a much bigger library of resources of how to feel and think about the world. I wanted some of that.

I came to the following conclusions about positive and negative emotions:

They are, for some people, the preferred way of paying attention to their experience.

They are a vital component of experience, but not primary data.
Although they seem to "just happen", emotions arise as the result of a very rapid and complex process in the mind.
They are messages about a value judgment that was made.
Emotional intensity reflects the importance that the issue holds for a person.
They provide the cause and direction for some people's behaviour.

HOW TO USE THIS BOOK

In this book I intend to share some counter-intuitive knowledge about emotions. Two friends are insisting I should call this book "Emotional Intelligence 3.0". In my approach to writing this book, I was confronted with some realities about my own and other people's emotions again and again: emotions, when decoded or understood, have logic of their own and it takes a kind of wisdom, an intuitive way of looking deeper and wider, to grasp the message(s) of an emotion. I am both the receiver and the creator of my emotions.

The power of emotional wisdom, and the competence to deal with your emotions in a respectful and effective manner is based on a new way of thinking about emotions (please refer back to the six points at the bottom of the Preface section). One such difference is to be "inside the emotion" as it happens to you, rather than as an observer, and yet knowing you also have the option to step out of the experience of the emotion. And then, when you do need to take on the role of an observer, how do you do it in a way that is respectful of your experience, and leads to a meaningful way of living with the emotions that rule your life? This is not an easy task. This distancing – the observer position – implies a looking in, and this is typically the position advocated by the EQ-experts. Under normal circumstances however, both the speed and the intensity with which emotions happen make it very difficult to move into this observer position. And this is where I hope that the techniques I offer in this book may be useful for you to use to overcome the dual challenge of speed an intensity. Failing that, however, you may need to ask a therapist or a coach to help with the words for, and understanding of, the message of your emotions.

Since this is a new road map, with many counter-intuitive pieces of information, I recommend you start the journey with the first chapter.

In the first five chapters I have shared with you my take on what emotions are like from the inside and a different way of thinking about emotions. I have given you "the information", but I am also inviting you to test the information in and through your own experience.

Starting in chapter 1, "Emotional Self-Mastery", I answer the question why we need to bother to take notice of our emotions? There are many reasons, some of which are: emotions add meaning to our way of life, they give "texture" to our everyday living, and they make us aware of the meanings we live in. Most importantly: they are messages of an assessment we have made. They are the consequence of a judgement or comparison we have made from our experience.

Chapter 2 will help you to understand the subtlety of the messages of emotions. "How to Understand your Emotions". The aim is the meeting and coming together of heart and mind. This chapter will help you to come to grips with where emotions come from. You will come away with a knowing of what some of the processes are (the "how") that we run when we create our emotions.

Chapter 3 deals with what to do with your emotions. Here we explore when and how to do it in a way that helps us to overcome emotional restrictions. Overcoming emotional restrictions is a precondition to living a life that is closer to the best version possible for you.

Chapter 4, "Working with your Emotions", provides the cues to recognise how emotions are coded. This is useful not just to help you to name or recognise your emotions, but also to grasp how to change the emotion at the level of feelings rather than at the level of the meaning or message.

Chapter 5 deals with the specifics of how to change emotions with care, respect and to do it in an appropriate manner. This chapter is the heart of the book. Spending thorough time on this chapter, and getting comfortable with the process, is a good investment of time and energy.

Chapter 6 deals with listening to other people, and trust me, this is not regurgitating the old stuff on how to listen. To really hear what people are saying, is active, asking questions. Remembering the saying: words are unverified rumours.

Chapters 7-10 are about specific applications, so here you need only to read the parts that you feel you need.

Chapter 11 acts as a reminder of the good news and the rest of the feel-good library. In this chapter I merely touch on the benefits of using the whole feel-good library, and may I assure you there are many, and well-researched evidence, that you may rely on.

The emphasis (in the learning and tools contained in this book) is on understanding and working with your own emotions from the inside. The practical activities will be a great help. The two chapters on other people (Listening and Changing an Emotion) can help when you have a conversation about emotions with other people. If, however, you feel you are not making progress or if the intensity of the emotion is too high, then please contact a licensed therapist or qualified NLP-practitioner.

EMOTIONAL WISDOM

Emotions are such an integral part of being human that one can say that people live and die for their emotions. We all want to have the good life, and identify it with the experience called "happiness" or even more nebulously, being "fulfilled". A mother would die to protect a child whom she "loves" more than her own life. A person would put his life on the line to save a friend. Sometimes we dislike somebody so intensely that we can call it "hate" – some people are even prepared to kill because they "hate", and damn the consequences. People can get consumed by "guilt" over something that they had done, and for many, many years pick at this guilt like a sore. "Awe" has produced beautiful music, poetry, art and conversion to religion. Even if you do not consider the "big" ones, emotion plays a role daily in decision-making for many people: if you feel good about it, you do it; if you feel bad, you don't. Essentially, an emotion is an experience we strive for or try to repeat or avoid. This book you are about to read starts from the perspective that emotions reflect the intensity of meaning. There are two central ideas in this approach: Firstly, emotions have their own physical reality and point to a process that preceded the experience of the emotion. Secondly, emotions signify the intensity of what things mean to people – the more intense the emotion, the more meaningful it is for the person. This has a further implication: as long as the meaning stays the same, the emotions stay the same. We will explore this, and more, in this book.

Can emotions be intelligent?
When I started writing this book many years ago (1997), one question I intended to answer was "are the distinctions between feelings and emotions useful"? At the time, I had just read Daniel Goleman's book on emotions, Emotional Intelligence, and was so excited by this well-written and well-researched book, that I decided to expand on my own in-the-margin notes. It prompted me to write about my own thoughts about the subject of emotions. I came to the following conclusions, which I am sharing with the reader in much more detail in this book:
Emotions in themselves are not intelligent.
The distinction between emotions and feelings is not useful or clarifying, nor does it "add value" as the current saying in business goes. In fact, from here on, the use of the word emotions includes feelings.
Emotions are a bodily response to an internal or external event.
Emotions always have meaning, and these meanings are specific to the person and the context.

To understand an emotion, one has to ask questions about how the emotion arose. The emotion is not ever the answer; the intelligence of an emotion is "outside" of it. Emotions point to a meaning behind it, and if you don't refer to the meaning they point to, you won't be able to understand what an emotion is about.

Thought, which forms the content of an emotion, has a structure, and represents a process which can be understood and changed.

Intense emotions act like a magnet that draws thoughts that are like the emotion into the span of attention – which in itself is not bad, depending upon the context and the kind of emotion.

The Fad of Emotional Intelligence

Since Daniel Goleman introduced the concept of "emotional intelligence" to the popular market, the thinking about emotions has expanded progressively to include more and more non-emotional processes and content under the blanket name of "emotions". Riding on this expanded definition of "emotional intelligence" came the inevitable and increasing variety of techniques purporting to supply "the answer" to the good life. Once it was accepted that emotions include cognitive content, it opened the door to inputs about how one should, ideally, be emotionally intelligent.

In my experience, the problem with these courses and "right answer" approaches is that it adds issues and content to emotions which has confused, rather than clarify matters. "Managing your emotions" easily leaves the person who buys into this mode of thinking with the full-time job of being "that" kind of person with only "those" kinds of emotions.

The Alternative: Emotional Wisdom

This book offers an alternative:

How to be respectful of the spontaneous emotional response you have to an event.

How to learn from your emotions and explore alternative choices about expressing emotions, or changing the content of an emotion, when and if you need to.

How to understand that even though emotions are not carriers of intelligence, they offer important information about how you are in the world.

Emotions give vitality to living, which through the ages have been "reasons" for which people marry, fight wars, create beautiful art, etc. It therefore deserves more respect than being "managed" and shaped without respectfully understanding their messages, and what is good or not so good about them.

The best way to employ emotional control is to do it before emotions reach a high intensity. But even during some moments of high intensity, emotions can be brought back to useful levels of intensity or even changed with a step-by-step approach.

To change an emotion requires some thinking about the value of the emotion in the context, in other words, changing emotions require "ecology checks".

In short, this book is about understanding, and then doing according to the insights gained.

CHAPTER 1

EMOTIONAL SELF-MASTERY

Is it Possible?

What are emotions?

Key points about emotions:

1. They are, for some people, the preferred way of paying attention to their experience.
2. They are a vital component of experience, but not primary data.
3. Although they seem to "just happen", they actually arise as the result of a very rapid and complex process in the mind.
4. They are messages about a value judgement that was made.
5. Emotional intensity reflects the importance that the issue holds for a person.
6. They provide the cause and direction for some people's behaviour.

When you are in love, for instance, it is great to feel the emotion, and one can become very creative in finding derivative outlets for these incredibly pleasant feelings. Can you remember how it felt as if you loved with your whole body, sometimes so much that you felt you would burst? Wasn't it great?

But what a difference when you're hurting! You wish, with the same intensity as the experienced pain, that it would stop. You would at least consider (if not actually do) almost anything to make the hurt go away – including even pretending that you are not hurting. When you hurt, you wish you could believe, and do, what people say when they tell you to pay attention to something else, just to ignore "it", or to remember that "tomorrow" you will feel better, etc.

Have you noticed something in the two examples cited above? In both instances, you tend to pay attention to the external circumstances and believe that the emotions spring from outside of yourself. Not only does it seem like your emotional experience is "caused" by the event or person in that particular context, but also that you are at the receiving end of your emotions. In other words, your emotions just happen and you "get" a feeling.

How many poems can you think of where the poets wax lyrical about how things have changed since the loved one appeared in their lives? Not only does the "world" now appear to be a friendlier, warmer place, but most remarkable are the "neurological" changes that have happened in the people themselves, for instance, an increase in abilities:

"Before I met you, I was ________ and now, since I fell in love with you, I am a different person, thanks to you in my life!"

When a person hurts, one may observe a similar way of thinking about one's hurt. For example, you must have actually heard somebody say in anguish, "Why did they die and just leave me like this? I am angry that they can just leave me like this! I thought they loved me! Now that they're dead, how do they expect me to cope without them?"

Because hurt is so unpleasant, some people prefer not to pay attention to it or pretend it did not happen. The effort not to pay attention to hurt is an attempt to reduce the hurt by reducing awareness of it, but this strategy comes at a cost.

Pain, the message that something is wrong, will stay for as long as the message is valid. But then, this can be said of all emotions: they stay available to be experienced as long as the "message" is valid.

Some would object to the above statement and say it is not true. When they compare it with their own experience, for example, of feeling creative, people could cite many instances of how creativity is not something you can control, that it is something that comes and goes, is unpredictable in its appearance, and frequently "just happens" without any apparent reason or cause. Or love, that it always mellows out over time and rarely maintains its intensity over time. Or grief that continues way beyond the time that is "normal" for most people. They then draw the conclusion that emotions last as long as they have to, and then they change or disappear; that they have their own rules and "comings and goings"; and that they are part and parcel of living, and you just have to accept them.

There is great misunderstanding about the nature of emotions, partly because we all experience them and consequently, consider ourselves to be experts about our own experience. This is compounded by the fact that most efforts to explain emotions have not contributed much to the clarification of what they are and how we can manage our emotions. They remain the enigma of experience, mainly due to two fallacies: Firstly, that emotions "just happen out of the blue", and secondly, that they are caused by events and people.

Because this book is about helping and not merely understanding, expect some thought teasers about your emotions that you can verify in your own experience. Let me challenge you at this point: remain sceptical until you find verification for these views in your personal experience.

There is an added advantage to taking up this challenge, and that is, by keeping track of your own emotions, you can build your own library of "coping strategies".

ACTIVITY:
Which emotions have you experienced during the past month? List the emotions in two columns: positive emotions in one, and negative emotions in another column. Try to make the list as complete as you can, even if an emotion was present only briefly or not very intensely. (If you have trouble remembering the emotions, think back on the events of the past month and recall which emotions you experienced before, during and after these events.)
How many positive, and how many negative emotions did you experience? What is your "feeling good"-ratio during this period?

Do you recognise a pattern when certain emotions occur? This question brings the "when" into focus to help you to develop awareness of which messages you experience in which situations and/or contexts. Please note if there is a pattern when the emotions occur. Let's say, for example, that before you even have a meeting with person X, you already find yourself wondering what is going to go wrong. This anticipation of "wrong", even if it may be justified, might very well create a certain expectation and, along with it, form part of a self-fulfilling prophecy. Now, upon reflection, can you balance the emotions by thinking of another message and experience that might be more useful to you than this one?

Emotions are Messages
Emotions are messages to yourself, about yourself. The fascinating thing about an emotion or an emotional experience is the fact that the emotion itself carries no content. An emotion becomes "complete" when the thoughts that "go with" the feeling become part of the awareness. This is when a feeling starts to make sense, because the person now recognises or understands what the feeling is about, what it is aimed at, or what it is a reflection of. Therefore, if thoughts are a requirement for emotions to be complete, it implies that feelings/emotions are actually the body's response to what the mind does.

Emotions are therefore not primary information, but reflect preceding thought processes, namely of giving meaning to something in the mind. Please note that "not primary" is not the same as saying that they are not important. On the contrary, emotions provide very important information about what things mean to us. They are also crucial to the ability to recognise this meaning, specifically whether this meaning is positive or negative, liked or disliked, favourable or unfavourable, etc. A great number of people, for instance, "test" whether a decision is a good or not based on how they feel about the decision. Checking how you feel about something can be called doing a feeling test. People with a preference for doing "feeling tests" would therefore have internal recognition systems that allow them to recognise feeling signals for "yes", "no", or "uncertain". They have a definitive signal for at least "yes" and "no" and, until they feel the message, they "cannot" decide.

Another "function" of emotions is that they provide a status report of sorts that reflects the experienced condition of your emotional well-being. When your internal experience is that you as a person, and/or your experience of your circumstances meet with internal criteria, then you will experience a positive emotion. However, if your assessment is that you or your circumstances are not meeting these internal criteria, then your non-acceptance will express itself as a negative or unpleasant emotion.

Equally, emotions reflect your self-assessment. If you meet your internal criteria for your own behaviour, then you will feel good about yourself. Not meeting your criteria will lead to guilt. Not meeting somebody else's criteria leads to shame.

The French philosopher, Jean-Paul Sartre, succinctly described emotions as "the embodiment of meaning" in his work A Sketch for a Theory of the Emotions. This is a useful description, because the rational part of the mind does the meaning-giving, and this meaning is then expressed in the body as an emotion or feeling. This also applies to "gut feelings", where meaning is experienced, although the words have not yet penetrated the awareness; you know that you know, but you cannot precisely formulate it yet; or you know that you know something, but at this time you do not know what that "something" is yet.

The Meaning of Emotions

The process of ascribing meaning to an experience happens so rapidly in the brain that some philosophers and psychologists refer to meaning as a "given" of experience. And if I say rapidly, I mean rapidly. Take, for example, when you listen to a person, your experience is that you hear them instantaneously, not so? Not only do you hear them immediately, but you are also simultaneously aware of your opinion about what you have just heard. Now, here is the marvel: in order for you to hear and have an opinion, your mind had to perform a vast number of neurological processes outside of your awareness for you to have reached this point. Let me mention some of the things that your mind has to do in order for you to understand and have an opinion about what you have listened to: your brain had to compare the words you heard with what is in its data bank to recognise them; it had to give the understanding meaning by doing some of the following multitude of comparisons:

do I have previous experience that is relevant to this issue? Was it pleasant or not? How does this match with my values? Was it said in a way that enables me to trust the message?

What does the message really mean (comparing the syntax of the language structure)? Is this true or not (compared to what I know, or how I "read" this person)? I don't know how many hundreds or even thousands of comparisons and distinctions people make before they arrive at an understanding and an opinion about what they hear, but the point is, it all happens during your "instantaneous" hearing, recognising and judging of the message.

Emotions "just (seems to) happen" because the brain processes information so rapidly that emotions are the tail end of a process, the "left-overs" of our thinking, as it were.

ACTIVITY:

Here is a way for you to explore how incredibly fast the brain can process information and give meaning to it. Think of a time when you were listening to an interesting talk or a discussion (please think about an event that really happened to you so that you can make a "real life life test"). From memory, recall what was said and specifically your opinion at the time, namely whether you agreed or not. Your experience of agreement or disagreement could have been in the form of seeing something in your mind, or you could have been talking to yourself, or you might have had an awareness of a particular feeling.

Some people become aware of their opinions through a combination of all three the mentioned sensations. How did you become aware of your opinion in the example you had to think about – pictures, sounds, feelings or a combination of these?

Here is what your brain had to do for you to have to become aware of your own opinion. As you hear a sentence, your brain firstly pays attention to the words and "checks" whether they are recognised; then the sentence is analysed in terms of the syntax to understand the meaning of the words, following which the "non-verbal packaging" (i.e. the subtle meaning being communicated by the unspoken part of the message, which carries 93% of the meaning of the words) is analysed to complete the meaning-giving part of the analysis.

This analysis of the subtle meaning will have a sequence of comparative steps in which the meaning is compared with previous experience and meanings. Based on this comparison, the person will know/recognise the meaning, or if the signals are unclear, contradictory or unknown, experience confusion, which will lead to further individual processes in an effort to remove the discomfort of this particular emotion.

Now, here is the crunch and please check this against your own experience: One experiences that all of this happens instantaneously as you hear – you understand immediately, and have a ready opinion in your mind, or you know instantly that you are confused. There is absolutely no delay in your experience of what you hear, see or feel. It has an immediate representation in your mind, even though all the modalities (that is, your experience of the picture, sound, feeling, smell and taste components in your awareness) might not be in your consciousness at that particular moment of paying attention.
Another feature of the meaning-giving process is that the meaning an incident has for the person is more important than the reality of the incident. Let me explain this with the internal process that happens when somebody gets criticised and their response is one of hurt. If you can clearly remember a time when you have been criticised and experienced the "hurt" or the sting of the words, then you might not at first agree with my next statement. Keeping in mind the speed with which the brain processes information, you might not be aware of this, but it is not so much the words that hurt (how can they?) but it is what I add to the words that "causes" the hurt. Test this for yourself. If I called you "a car" to your face, you most probably would not even give it a second thought. Why? Because you would (very, very rapidly) have done an internal comparison and know that this comment cannot be applicable to you, therefore you would summarily discard it as not about you at all, and your emotional response would be like your internal judgement – neutral, or wanting to laugh, or confusion about what am I getting at. Thus, when criticism does hurt, you have added a meaning or a reality to the comment that gives it the value of being hurtful. Additions like: "it is true", "they say that because they do not respect me," and "they are supposed to love me," will guarantee a painful experience every time.

This principle is also applicable to more serious events that people experience. It is what the event means to someone that causes an experience of trauma. The meaning of the event plays a role that is more important than the event itself.

The issue of "objectivity" becomes an interesting one if you consider that the meaning-giving process happens so rapidly that it can only happen unconsciously, as in, "outside of awareness" (the conscious mind works at the speed of a very rapid talk-rate). The author is very tempted to offer that "objectivity" is a wish that the brain is not capable off.

Emotion as an attention-getter

One reason you pay so much attention to an emotion is because it can be so intrusive in your consciousness that it can get a value in consciousness that gives it a primary importance, or that it becomes a priority message in what you pay attention to. For an emotion to "get the attention" it has to become intense enough for the mind to pay attention to it. It seems that every individual has their own threshold for emotions, both to pay attention to, as well as an internal definition for "enough".

You may have noticed, from your experience, that some people pay frequent attention to their own emotions. These people would also make constant reference to how they or other people are feeling. The important information that they pay attention to is how people feel about things, or who felt what in a particular situation. Their vocabulary also has many references to feeling-words. They seem to have a preference for paying attention to feeling information, more so than to the other kinds of information that make up experience, like what things looked like, or what they sounded like.

This preference is, however, a relative preference and not to be thought of as a typology: in other times and places the same people might have a preference to pay attention to the other components of experience, like what they saw or heard, what people said or what they were saying to themselves in their minds. Whatever they were paying attention to, or whatever the distinctions and comparisons are that they were making in a particular situation, will determine how they pay attention to it.

ACTIVITY:

Think back and try to get a sense of your preferred ways of paying attention in different situations. Use a few of the following examples, and follow the pattern of the holiday example:

Think of a highlight from your last holiday.

Think of the context: what happened in that moment, where did it happen, when did it happen (in your whole holiday: when specifically) and who was involved in that moment with you? These questions are to give you a sense of the boundary for this highlight.

As you now think of that event, how are you most aware of it: in feeling (kinesthetic), sound, picture, smell or taste form? The duration that you spend on this modality will indicate your preference.

Other examples:

- Mastering a new skill; grasping a new concept;
- Discovering a new positive about yourself.

- Discovering a new positive about your child, partner, friend, business colleague.
- Entering a new, or your favourite, restaurant.
- Buying something special: book, clothing, gift.

Some thoughts on "enough": the decision of "having had enough" is a critical step in how the mind turns a painful event into a traumatic experience. Interviews that I have conducted with people who have experienced trauma from a variety of experiences, consistently show that the experience for them had been "more than they can handle" and that it was this aspect of the experience that was the final straw for them. One hears the same thing from people who had endured certain experiences over a period of time and then suddenly "reached their limit" and gave up, gave in, or as the popular expression goes, "had a nervous breakdown".

Emotionally sensitive people

We all know people who describe themselves as "emotionally sensitive". This designation is often viewed negatively since these people seem to demand extra emotional care that some people may not be ready or willing to give. Furthermore, they are known for their intense responses to incidents that other people might consider being excessive or inappropriate for the event.

Here is a way to understand what may be happening. To the extent that you pay more attention to your emotions, you become more sophisticated with the distinctions you make concerning your feelings. Being able to make more distinctions implies a proficiency that includes an early awareness of your emotions, in other words, the threshold for emotions to register in your awareness, is lower.

It is, however, also true that people can become so aware of their emotions that they can get "stuck" in them, meaning that their attention becomes so fixated on the feeling that they cannot shift their attention way from it and pay attention to something that is not related to that particular emotion. Their emotions become like a magnet for thoughts that are similar to the emotions.

You might recognise this in your own life: when you have one of those days that you "get out of bed with the wrong foot", it seems like every event for the rest of the day is a reinforcement of that feeling. It is not so much what happens as how you were feeling to start off with. When you jump out of bed feeling like you "can't wait to get started", nothing can faze you or even slow you down. We can all be "magnetised" by our emotions when we experience them at a certain level of intensity.

"Emotionally sensitive" people seem to experience this level of sensitivity sooner, and more often.

One other feature of "getting stuck" in an emotion is that a person might then experience it as an end state, instead of as a message to respond to. This state of affairs leads to thoughts that seem to go in a loop that feeds on itself, and the person seems unable to get to the next step, namely, making a decision about what to do in response to their messages to themselves.

What is the message?

At this stage you might be very curious about what these messages are that emotions communicate. These messages are not only unique to each individual, but they are also very specific to the person's assessment in a particular situation or context.

There is a saying that "the map is not the territory". Up to now this is exactly the point, namely, your experience of an event is from a place where your brain has added your very personal stamp to that event. Your brain interprets the event with whatever experiences it already has available from your own history and the features that make you unique. When two people have to describe the same event, you often get fairly dissimilar descriptions and interpretations because their brains function differently and they therefore paid attention to different things and experienced the meaning of the event in their own distinctive way.

One of the most active filters in the brain is the values filter. "Filters" are the way the different functions in the brain combine to analyse and interpret the information that is being processed during an experience. Specifically, a "filter" is what the information stored in each of these areas is called, and has the function of contributing to the brain's understanding and processing of a specific neurological event. A "filter" is stored information that contributes to the process of giving meaning to the neurological event or the experience (as we have been calling it up to now).

Your values filter is your set of criteria against which you judge an event in terms of right/wrong, should/shouldn't, etc. It is the domain of morals from which human beings assess the world around them. This is not about the rightness of anybody's values, but the reason why we pay attention to values, or criteria, as I will henceforth call it, is because as a filter, it has a very powerful effect on the content and meaning we ascribe to an experience. Your criteria filter largely operates unconsciously, and at an incredible speed, and as we have seen previously, you only become aware of the tail-end of the evaluation process in the form of having a ready-made judgement about something. Only when it is required, like when you get asked or confronted, do you consciously pay attention to your criteria in a particular situation. Otherwise, you mostly operate with an unconscious criteria base.

Our criteria are products of our social conditioning and typically acquired through your personal history, and learnt from parents, teachers, religion, culture and other significant people or influences in your life. Because they are unconscious, they are rarely updated. The updating of criteria only happens under fairly specific circumstances, like when they are not appropriate any longer, or when you have progressed to another set of values, or if you are confronted by the fact that they are not functioning in your best interest, etc. The minimum condition for criteria change is an awareness of the criteria with a distinct discomfort about the inappropriateness of the particular set of criteria. Let me add hastily, this is not the discomfort of knowing you are out of step with your own values, experienced as a strong message from your conscience.

One more thing about criteria: contrary to what many psychologists believe, the criteria that shape your experience are context specific. People do not operate from long lists of criteria, nor do they have "a value system" because every experience, including the criteria that operate in them is context specific.
One can therefore say that your criteria determine how you pay attention in the world – and give meaning to the world – in a way that may or may not correspond with what other people would consider the meaning to be. Ergo, "the map is not the territory".

ACTIVITY:
Here is how you can verify for yourself that criteria are context specific and few in number. Think of a real example of "trusting" somebody. In order for you to notice how criteria influence experience, please be specific about the time when the trusting happened by thinking about a particular person, a time and place that would be a good example of trusting that person.

Notice also, what you would call this particular kind of friend (this is part of the context-specific data), in other words, a close friend, a long-standing friend, an intimate friend, etc.

As you think about the example of trusting this person, answer one or more of the following questions (they are variations on a theme and will get the same information, except certain questions would make more sense):
- What is important to you in this example?
- What do you pay attention to as you think about this example?
- What do you want from this person now as you think about trust?
- What is significant to you in thinking about this example?

To compare this information, think of somebody else in a different category of friendship and answer the same questions. You will notice some of the following:

- You might use the same words, but if you were to arrange them in order of priority, they would have different priorities.
- The same words would be recognised in different ways if you were to think of "how would you know?"
- That you would spontaneously think of about three to five criteria words according to which you would judge "trust."

Emotions are the result of this assessment of yourself, other people, and/or the world. Feelings are the message of the outcome of this criteria judgement. When the judgement is favourable, the feelings will be pleasant, while a negative judgement will produce an unpleasant feeling.

In conclusion: Emotions are the tail-end of an incredibly rapid meaning-giving process. Individuals have unique ways of recognising the importance of their own emotions. People differ in terms of how they make distinctions about their emotions with a resultant difference of the "when" – when they notice emotions, when they "magnetise" their thoughts, and when emotions become too much. A person recognises the meaning of a particular event as the result of a value judgement through the accompanying emotion. The minimum distinction the person would make is favourable/unfavourable, like/dislike, right/wrong, etc.

CHAPTER 2

HOW TO UNDERSTAND YOUR EMOTIONS

The Structure of Emotions

In this chapter I acknowledge Leslie Cameron-Bandler and Michael Lebeau, for their book **Emotional Hostage: Rescuing Your Emotional Life** (available at Amazon.com), which I consider to be the most profound book I have read on the topic of emotions.

Recognising the structure of your Emotions

How do you recognise your own emotions? This might, at face value, seem like a strange question to ask, let alone answer. It is, however, not only relevant for this book, but also in our everyday lives. Have you noticed how people are nowadays making fewer and fewer distinctions about which emotions they experience daily?

ACTIVITY:

To explore this for yourself: list how many emotions you have experienced today (during the course of the day, up to this point).

You might notice that you possibly only come up with one or two emotions, and that it could also seem as if the same emotion, or maybe two or three emotions, repeat themselves. Think back on what you have read in the previous chapter about how emotions reflect judgements according to your criteria, and remember that you probably make those judgements at the rate of many thousands a day, one for each context or situation you experience. Make a list of all the different events or situations you have experienced today, up to this point, and assess (or even guess) whether each one had a positive or negative effect on you, the people involved or what it shows you about the world as reflected by each event. Now compare this to the information you have about your emotions throughout the day.

You would probably find that the events of lesser importance tend to reflect that opinion or judgement in a mild or non-intense emotion. Events that really matter would have a decidedly stronger emotion accompanying it. Furthermore, events that have a positive or beneficial effect on you, your life, and/or your relationship with other people or the world, will be confirmed by a positive or pleasant emotion. The reverse would apply to an experience where your judgement is that your criteria have not been met.

If you compare what you now know about your emotions to when you started the exercise, you will notice how you are subsequently more aware of the range and nuances of your emotions. So instead of a monochrome picture, your emotional life might more accurately be described as a kaleidoscope of vibrant colours in an ever-changing mixture of patterns, reflecting the richness of your internal aliveness. This incredible variety can be thought of as the colours in a sequence of experiential maps a person moves through in a day.

This comparison illustrates the point we started off with, namely how most people make very few (and fairly simple) emotional distinctions and therefore lose out on valuable information about the way they think about their relationship with themselves, other people, and the world.

The loss of accurate emotional information is further exacerbated by the confusion we create when we misname our emotions (that would normally reflect our judgements according to our criteria for particular experiences) and inappropriately link them to objects – like when you say you "love" ice-cream or the latest model of a luxury car.

Experiential Logic

Consider the topic of experiential logic as a synonym for emotional wisdom. Emotional wisdom is the ability to understand emotions in terms of the logic of the emotional experience. It is the ability to grasp or understand, appreciate and exercise choice regarding experiential logic. The way you make distinctions about the emotions you experience does not correlate with your physiology at all, but still gives you valid information about which emotions you are experiencing. Before you do an exercise to help you establish the validity of the next point, here is one more piece of information to consider, and that is that our internal experience operates with a kind of logic that is not linear, or "scientific". When we attempt to understand events or happenings in nature, in the external world, we typically to use a cause-and-effect way of thinking through which we ask what caused a phenomenon or speculate about the effect something will have. But the logic of the internal world doesn't necessarily work in the same way. This internal logic, or "experiential logic" as I call it, is difficult to define with words, but I will give descriptive examples to get the concept across.

Look, for example, at how children create the imaginary worlds they play in. Often, in their play, children create a world of imaginary monsters that they're fighting or running away from and, at some point, come rushing in, shrieking, looking for affirmation from the adults that there are, in fact, not really monsters lurking behind the trees in the garden. They often get so carried away with the reality of their game that they need somebody else's verification that "it's just a game". While they play, and for the duration of the game, this imaginary world they created is as real as anything else.

It is, however, not only children who create these alternate "realities". Adults can very comfortably talk themselves into the same kinds of unreal "realities" that may be more subtle, sophisticated and complex, but equally compelling and mentally occupying. Adults can also, therefore, create worlds they "play in", even though some of these games can be very painful and psychologically devastating. While this game is being played, and the player is "in" it, these games are what reality is made up of; it really becomes their reality, not a figment of their imagination.

If, at this, stage you notice the parallels with one's dream experience, congratulations to you, for you have identified one of the key characteristics of this "experiential logic". Like dreams, one is not completely at the mercy of this logic; it can be changed, updated, interrupted and/or reviewed for adjustment. But, and this is an important "but", this is the map (not the territory) the person is operating from. Under the circumstances, it is the best they can do, given "the map", or the reality they are in. Unless they add a step in their experience of this map and ask a question about the map, they cannot review or consider changes to this map.

This updating of one's maps is an experience we are all familiar with and is generally referred to as "personal growth". Contrary to some popular and professional views, not all updating has to be painful or happen over an extended period of time, as you can verify from your own experience.

Just like the "rules" of our inner experience have a code of their own (irrespective how much it overlaps with other peoples' maps), our recognition of our emotions has a similar private code that does, however, overlap somewhat with those of other people.

Kinesthetic Cues for Recognising Emotions

The key question is this: how do you and your brain recognise an emotion, especially the variety that is possible given the many criteria-distinctions that your brain continuously makes? Whether you pay attention to it or not, how does your brain make this incredible number of fine distinctions?

There are basically two ways, namely through cues in your body and the internal structure of the emotions themselves. Firstly, bodily or "Kinesthetic" cues. (The word "Kinesthetic" refers to distinctions you make in your body about emotions or feelings.) What happens inside your head are thoughts, but what you sense or feel in your body are emotions; there has to be a certain amount of physiological change in your body for "it" to have sufficient value to penetrate your conscious mind. And herein lies a fascinating mystery about how the human mind works, specifically its way of distinguishing emotions.

ACTIVITY:

Every emotion has its own "code" in your body, which is your way of recognising what emotion you are experiencing at any specific moment. So now, do one of the following:

a) For a moment, consider what emotion you are experiencing as you are reading this.

b) Alternatively, think of something you experienced a short while ago that you can still remember clearly. Imagine that you are back in that event as if it is happening right now. Think about who is involved, what you see, what you hear people say, or which noises you hear, and what you are feeling.

Now, regardless of whether you have chosen a) or b), do this exploration:
Give the emotion you are experiencing a name (it could be something like inquisitive, interested, attentive, happy, relaxed, etc.) The more specific you can be with the identification, the better it is for the exercise. Avoid vague names or descriptions like good/bad or like/dislike.

Pay attention to how you recognise the emotion by asking and answering the following questions:
Close your eyes and try to establish where and how in your body you are experiencing the emotion? You will find you can recognise a place where a particular feeling is situated. If you have some difficulty with this, here are some examples of what people report: tension is experienced as a ball in the pit of the stomach, or as pressure that stretches across the forehead, or as a developing tightness across the chest, etc. Happiness has been described as an overall feeling that is larger than one's body, or as a tingling feeling in one's chest or stomach area, while some people report racing or fluttering of the heart, etc.

How big is the feeling?
What shape does the feeling have?
Is the feeling light or heavy?
Is the feeling steady and consistent, or pulsating?

Answer as many questions as you can, it is not important that you know the answer to all the questions.

Now repeat the exercise for another emotion and notice how the coding for each emotion is unique to the emotion (and also unique to you). Here is a summary of the steps:

Think of a time when you experienced an emotion you would like to get to know better.

Think of that time and imagine that it is happening to you in the present moment: what do you hear, see and feel during the event that is "now" happening to you?

As you are experiencing the event fully in the present, ask yourself the same questions as above, namely, where, how specifically, how big, light, consistent, etc. this new feeling is.

As you compare the two emotions with each other, how different or similar are your body cues or coding for the two emotions? You may, for instance, notice that the coding for positive emotions are more alike than when you compare positive and negative emotions with each other.

Interestingly, you may want to pay attention and observe that when people share their emotions with each other during a conversation, they often unconsciously point to where in their bodies they are experiencing a particular emotion.

Experiential Components of an Emotion
Criteria
The first component was dealt with in chapter 1, namely that an emotion is a message about your wellbeing. It reflects the decision you have made concerning your definition, according to your own criteria, for wellbeing. Therefore, the first component of the experience of an emotion is that the criteria against which the judgement is made are inherent in the experience of it.

Emotions are therefore not just things that happen to people or something that needs to be tolerated or ignored if it becomes "bothersome". It is actually important information about your internal processes, about what is significant to you, and even arguably, how distinctive you are in relation to other members of the group you belong to. (This is an important point in reference to how we listen to other people's messages about their emotions, because it is so easy to make assumptions about "why" people are hurting in a particular situation. One can only make assumptions based on one's own experience. Your experience might, or might not, be the same as the person to whom you are listening. Whatever the differences are, those are exactly the differences you have to listen for carefully, otherwise you would, in effect, be giving yourself the best advice you know how. More about this in the chapter on "listening").

Some other qualities of an (unpleasant) emotion:
Intensity
For most part, we make three decisions about our emotions, namely when to pay attention to them, when they are manageable and/or pleasant to the point of doing behavioural things to prolong the experience, and when they are "too much" and our behaviour and thinking are aimed at making it stop, change or go away. These are three different degrees of intensity that influence our responses to our emotional database.

Research hasn't yet been able to pinpoint which physiological changes have to take place for an emotion to reach an individual's threshold for them to pay attention to it, but from experience it is clear that paying attention to one's emotions is part of how one perceives the total "map" or experience.

In some circumstances, you would be more sensitive to your emotions, while in other circumstances less sensitive – this is called a relative preference of your attention. For instance, in some situations you could be so busy thinking in pictures or paying attention to sounds with your mind, that your emotions have to be much more intense before they can penetrate your consciousness.

Whatever you would pay attention to most during that moment will be your "relative preference". It does not mean that the other information (i.e. pictures, sounds, or feelings) "go away"; they are still available to experience by merely switching your attention to them; in terms of relative preference, it simply means that they are not the preferred information in your consciousness in this "psychological moment". If you have a preference for kinesthetic information, you would pay attention to your kinesthetic experience much more readily than when it is not your preference.

This preference is called a "relative preference" because it will not only shift from context to context, but also as you shift what you pay attention to. People's preferences are therefore relative to what they pay attention to at any given time.

When you pay attention to the kinesthetic part of your experience, and it still has a manageable intensity (as defined by you), then you can exercise your choice as to what to do about your experience of this event. If pleasant, you will most probably think of ways to prolong it (like getting married to the "source" of that kinesthetic experience). If unpleasant, your choice could be anything from ignoring it, or doing something to change the experience, or doing something related to the "source" of the experience.

When it reaches the next level of intensity, the kinesthetic part of the experience becomes like a magnet and "draws" to it pictures and sounds that, in content, are similar to the emotion. Sadness begets sadness, anger feeds on itself, worry gives birth to more of the same, etc. Thank your brain for having the same rules for positive and negative emotions: when you are happy, you smile at everybody; when you are relaxed, you see colours everywhere you look; when you are in love, everything is a reminder of the person you love. Needless to add that the more intense the emotion, the more magnetic it becomes and the more difficult it is for the person to "snap out" of the emotion they are caught up in. Their thinking spirals into a loop where the previous thought leads to the next thought, which is similar in content.

Furthermore, the number of internal events lessens. It is as if every single thought (whether in picture or sound form) just leads back to the same kinesthetic experience, no matter how hard they try to think of something else, and regardless what they think about, they almost instantaneously end up in the same place. It is a circular pattern of feeling–thought–feeling–thought–feeling–feeling–etc.

Time frame
Every emotion has an automatic time reference (past, present, future) built into the experience. Let's take a few random examples and, as you think about that emotion, notice where, in terms of time, your thoughts go to:

EMOTION	TIME FRAME
Guilt	You will go and fetch an event from the past, because guilt is typically an emotion about the past.
Anxiety	When you are anxious about something, your thoughts go into the future because that is where the event that you are concerned about will lie in wait for you.
Excitement	Present into the future; future.
Relaxed	Present.
Happiness	Present.
Fear	Remembering something from the past, imagining it is present, and thinking about future recurrence.

The Kinesthetic part of an experience is always in real time, meaning it is experienced in the present moment – in the here and now. The thought content, however, will have its own particular "place in time", that is, in the past, present, or future.

One of the features of experiential logic is the ability to think of an event from your past, and do it in such a way that you forget that it actually happened in the past. Because of the real-time character of emotions, the thoughts that go with them take on the same here-and-now quality.

When people get involved in the Kinesthetics of a past experience, they can become so engrossed that they forget that they are in the here and now, but are fully in the there-and-then of the original event.

We say people have "flash-backs" when they involuntarily recall very painful events from the past. When people have these intense experiences about the past, two things happen:
- Firstly, they forget that they are remembering and are not experiencing the original experience.
- Secondly, because they are in real time, they also forget some basic truths such as that they have survived the experience and have since grown as a person and now have skills and capabilities available to them which they did not have then, etc.

One of the tests for whether a person has completed the processing of a trauma from the past is that when they think about it again, they remain rooted in the here and now, fully conscious that they are recalling something from memory and now have the advantage of additional skills and circumstances that were not available to them then.

Merging
This is when the mind puts everything into one mental basket, the cumulative weight of which is experienced as being "too much". This not-helpful process is what leads to people considering suicide: all the things that go wrong, even if they are of lesser importance or not even related to the "big" one, get lumped together and this experience of "total hopelessness" and "uselessness" leaves them with the only acceptable option in the form of suicide.

The trap here is the merging of all the negatives into one experience which, in terms of its sheer psychological impact, could exceed the person's sense of it being within his/her control. This is one of the preconditions for a person to experience stress: even events which would otherwise not be considered stressful now become supporting evidence of how wrong things, are. The person then starts to pay attention to what is wrong, to the exclusion of the exceptions to the rule, and their "whole day is a disaster, one thing after the other just went wrong".

Two important issues need to be raised here:

- Firstly, what you pay attention to determines the reality you live in. People who experience intense stress or who have acute emotional pain, pay attention to information that is similar to their emotions and the opposites or exceptions just do not register. Their total experience is a verification of their hurt and stress, because internally they keep on "looping back" to experiences that affirm their emotion.

- Secondly, that which could give hope or at least allow them to qualify the extent of the negative experience, does not register sufficiently in their awareness and doesn't seem real enough for the person to temper their intense negative experience. "The difference that will make the difference" is not paid attention to, because the intensity of the unpleasant emotion is what determines "reality".

The merging of negative thinking is what "makes the whole world bad".

Tempo

Tempo concerns the speed at which you experience your thoughts running through your mind. During times of stress, for instance, the tempo of thinking is experienced as very fast and "too much", and this perception of a hastened or frenetic thought tempo contributes to the discomfort of the experience. In times of sadness, on the other hand, your thought processes can feel very slow and heavy, as if you become engulfed in it.

The common thread in these two examples is that the thought tempo – too fast or too slow – itself becomes uncomfortable and unacceptable to the person, which contributes to the unpleasantness of the experience.

> **ACTIVITY:**
>
> Put yourself into a very comfortable and relaxed state of mind. Without disturbing the flow of the experience, allow a part of your mind to pay attention to the tempo of your thoughts, then just go back to relaxing some more.
>
> After a while, allow your thoughts to gently speed up as if there is a slight sense of urgency to them and notice what happens to your emotion of relaxation.

Association

Association is when you are "in" the experience. In this context, when you are paying attention to what it is you are seeing, you are watching the world through your own eyes; in other words, you are the starting point of your observation, and the world is in front of you.

When you are dissociated, however, you watch as if you are a part of the scene; you can see your reaction as if you are watching a movie with you as a participant in it.

Typically, with issues that matter, or are important to the person, they would be so "in" the experience that for them, it is all that exists; any suggestions that things will pass, or that it is not all that bad, does not make sense because they are completely absorbed in the moment of the experience. For them to consider the options you are mentioning to them, means they have to be in the same dissociated position as you, otherwise this alternative perspective would not be relevant to their experience, and they would not be able to identify with it.

How associated or dissociated you are also has an impact not only on the intensity of the experience, but also on the "kind" of emotion you would then be experiencing. When you are associated, the tendency would be for the emotion to be more intense and consuming.

When you look at an event from a dissociated position, not only would you tend to not have the same intense emotion, but you will have an emotion about the event as opposed to what is happening to you in the event.

Being in a "meta-position" puts you in a judgemental position where your feelings will reflect your opinion about the event as opposed to your direct experience of the event. For example, your anger will be about what is happening in the event (a righteous anger) instead of anger that results from a personal, first-hand experience of hurt.

One of the preconditions of trauma is that an event is recalled and experienced in an associated way, meaning that the person is, at that point in time, not able to dissociate and get an alternative perspective for managing the event more effectively, rather than just desperately trying to survive.

In order for people to learn new ways of thinking about experiences, it is helpful if they can dissociate appropriately, so that they can learn about the alternatives instead of being caught up in the experience.

ACTIVITY:

Think of an experience of mild intensity that had enough of an impact on you to consider it worthwhile sharing it with a friend. As you think of this mildly intense experience by yourself, notice whether you are involved and seeing things through your own eyes, or whether you are dissociated?

Imagine sharing it with somebody right now, and notice whether you shift from being associated to dissociated?

If you do shift, notice how the content of your emotion changes and even maybe the intensity of the original emotion.

Take a moment to think about a person whom you care for, and specifically your last encounter. If you want to learn something from the event that may make your next encounter even more pleasant, look at the event as if you were watching a movie and give your movie character-self advice about some innovative possibilities.

Compare how difficult the same activity would be if you were remembering the event as if it was happening to you right now, and you could hear and see this person as if they were sitting in front of you.

In conclusion: Knowing something about the structure of an emotion puts us in a position to consider responsible ways of changing our minds. Emotions have a structure that is both felt and lived. The structure is how we subjectively recognise an emotion and how we can then explore its message. This structure is like an access code that gives us entry to the experiential logic of the emotion. This is the first step and provides us with respectful and responsible ways to change our emotions when we choose to do so.

CHAPTER 3

OPTIONS

What to do with Your Emotions

The good and bad news

The meanings of and ways of changing your emotions are now potentially available to you. Let us briefly review the function of emotions so that you can use the understanding to respectfully and ecologically change an emotion.

- Emotions are not primary information, but rather messages about your wellbeing.
- Emotions are the result of a judgement process: comparing internal events with your criteria.
- Changing emotions entail activating a new process of judgement or comparison.
- Emotions are an important source of information about yourself and the status of your internal experience.
- Even though the emotional message might seem simple, the process that precedes it is very complex and very rapid.

Emotional control, such as changing the content or intensity of an emotion, opens up fascinating ways for discovering what it means to be human, as well as ways to improve your quality of life. Before we get to emotional mastery, it is useful to further explore the topic of "emotional intelligence".

Emotional Intelligence

In his book, Emotional Intelligence: Why It Can Matter More Than IQ (Bloomsbury Publishing, London; 1996), Daniel Goleman gives a good summary of the thinking on the topic. The concept of emotional intelligence was largely created by Howard Gardner, who made a convincing case for multiple intelligences (seven to be precise), one of which is intelligence concerning your ability to make emotional distinctions. Goleman, however, lists the following five attributes that describe "emotional intelligence":

- Knowing your emotions.
- Managing emotions.
- Motivating yourself
      (marshalling emotions in the service of a goal).
- Recognising emotion in others.
- Handling relationships. Brief notes on each:

Knowing your emotions means recognising an emotion as it happens.

This implies two important distinctions:

- Firstly, the ability to become aware of the emotion as a cue to significant information about the ongoing event.
- Secondly, the ability to recognise what the message is, in other words, to distinguish the "content name" of the emotion, i.e. is it fear, anxiety, etc.

Recognising the kind or version of the emotion means you are identifying the message accurately.

Managing your emotions is about what you do with them internally. The term used is "handling" the emotions and refers to a broad range of options in experience, such as your internal strategies for dealing with the intensity of an emotion, what you do not to get "stuck" in an emotion, how you prevent an intense emotion from "overpowering" you, how you express the emotion in terms of appropriateness, etc.

Managing Emotions

Managing your emotions is really just another way of talking about emotional self-mastery. It is important to note that good emotional self-mastery is not the same as "not having" an emotion, denying an emotion, or avoiding situations so that you do not have to have the emotion in the first place. This is what emotional self-mastery is not.

It is, rather, the ability and the choice to express your emotions. Specifically, it means that you understand the message of your emotion and can then decide what to do with your experience of the emotion. When will you respond to the message of the emotion? How will you respond? Will you express the emotion verbally or nonverbally? Etc.

Self-motivation

When you motivate yourself emotionally, it refers to how you marshal or use your emotions in the service of a goal. This raises an interesting point, namely, that emotions or feelings are frequently an internal test of whether you are ready to do something or not.

More specifically, and please compare this with your own internal experience, people often use how they feel as a determining factor in deciding whether to do or not to do, as well as which "direction" (toward or away from) to behave in.

For example: if some people do not "feel motivated" they cannot get started; or if they don't get a good feeling, it is a "no" answer; or if it does not feel important, it is not; or if I don't feel I love you anymore, I cannot be married to you any longer; or if I feel good about something, it is reason enough to go ahead and do it; etc.

However, it is important to note that not everyone uses emotional tests to make go or no-go decisions. Some people use other decision-making strategies as regularly and as effectively as the ones who prefer to make emotional or feelings-based decisions.

Equally, people who use their emotions as an important factor in their decision-making process can be as effective as those who use other strategies, despite professional and popular scepticism. Using feelings or emotions as a basis for decision-making is a preference and a habit, and requires as much appropriate skill or "intelligence" as any other strategy.

Self-motivation is therefore not solely dependent on your emotions, and people would differ in their emotional requirements for doing or starting a particular behaviour. For those people for whom emotions are an important test for doing or not doing, emotions would be a key motivator. The point is, if you do not use your emotions as a starting point, but prefer to use other strategies for becoming motivated, it is not necessarily a reflection of your emotional intelligence.

Recognising emotions in someone else
Empathy, another ability that builds on self-awareness, is a fundamental "people skill". This is true for the extent to which, in the circumstances, emotions are an important source of information for the person you are interacting with.

Should you endeavour to work with somebody else's emotions, you had better be very comfortable and sophisticated in dealing with your own; otherwise you cannot "hear" the emotional messages people are offering. I suggest that you do with other people's emotions what you would do with your own: the distinctions (or lack thereof) that you make in your own experience will most probably be the same as what you are capable of in dealing with those of other people.

To define this component of emotional intelligence more accurately: recognising the kind of emotion and its message in somebody else is what constitutes empathy and is an important people skill. This should be an important consideration when deciding to what extent to position yourself as a people helper.

If you are emotionally tone deaf regarding your own experience, rather stay away from helping others with their emotionally charged personal issues.

Handling relationships is a reflection of your skill in handling emotions in other people
Emotions are part of the package that makes up the person with whom you relate. The ease or difficulty with which you handle somebody else's emotions, especially if

it is an important preference to them in that particular context, will be reflective of your skilfulness in handling other people.

Emotional Self-mastery

Emotional self-mastery is how you use your emotional intelligence. A person with high emotional intelligence is not necessarily skilled in self-management, or in managing other people. High intelligence speaks to the potential, and not necessarily the application of it. In other words, a person can, but they do not necessarily do.

Emotional self-mastery takes emotional intelligence a step further, to how you apply it to yourself. Emotional self-mastery could simply be added to the list of attributes of emotional intelligence, although, in it's own right, it has four attributes, namely emotional expression, emotional self-management, emotional flexibility, and managing the effect of an emotion on your thinking processes or what you pay attention to.

Emotional expression

What you do with an emotion once it is in your span of attention is an important aspect of emotional self-mastery. The more intense an emotion, the more difficult it is not to express it in behavioural or verbal forms. This refers to one aspect of internal emotional control, namely exercising your option of how (and when) you want to express the emotion of the moment. This is, for some, an area of great confusion. Expressing an emotion and paying attention to an emotion does not refer to the same mental strategy.

Typically, people who have had a painful emotional experience that involved somebody else, would, as a protective mechanism, decide "not to feel like that again". Sometimes they would recklessly decide not to have emotions at all, or not to feel that intensely ever again. This, in effect, means that in the process of protecting themselves, they deny or suppress important information. It amounts to shooting the messenger.

This aspect of emotional self-mastery is about utilising the information (rather than imagining that you can beneficially delete it from your database), deciding on your internal response to the message, as well as what your outward response will be. This is, in fact, not as "robotic" or calculated as it may sound.

People I have spoken to who have good emotional control have a built-in "wait" response to any intense emotions. They have developed an "interruption pattern" for themselves so that they can pay attention to the message first. For them, it is an important criterion to know and then to develop a decision option before they respond.

This brings us to another fascinating fact about the mind: Because the mind codes experience in a context-specific way, you need to build that into your considerations for effective self-management. (Refer to the section on self-change to review how to apply this principle for effective change.)

Emotional Flexibility

People who are good at emotional self-control and yet still keep their spontaneity intact, have great clarity in their minds about which emotions get the "control treatment", and when. One can, therefore, define "emotional flexibility" as your ability to make the decision about which emotions to control under which circumstances, and with which emotions (where, when and with whom), it is a no-holds-barred situation.

People who are adept at it allow themselves to do what the mind naturally does, namely to sort experiential information into its context-specific categories. A key component in ecological emotional control is therefore the context-specific consideration, in exactly the same manner as this principle applies to self-change.

Because the when and what of emotions are outside of your immediate control, emotional flexibility is therefore about how and when you express your emotions, not if you will "have" them.

Emotional Effect

The when and what of an emotion is the result of processes in the brain that happen too rapidly for conscious awareness or control. You are merely the receiver of the result of this judgement process, so in a certain sense your emotions are "given" to you. However, once they register in your consciousness, you can activate your ability to control and change them. The initial content and intensity of your emotion is a "given", but your response to the "given" is under your control.

Specifically, once you have registered an emotion, your ability to choose can be activated. You can then choose the content (or message) that you consider appropriate, the appropriate intensity, and the duration of the emotion. (The practicalities of doing this will be discussed in later chapters.)

Emotional Management

Emotional management is "getting" the emotions you want to have and doing the things you know will "give" you the intended emotion. This is not a novel idea. It is a natural part of being human to do things because they feel good, or to do them because you know that it will give you a pleasant feeling afterwards. "Chasing an emotion" through what we do, or avoid, or think about is often a major motivation for what we choose to spend time or large amounts of money on. On the one hand, we have the tendency to make fewer and cruder distinctions in our emotions, while on the other, we pursue more of "whatever feels good".

This tendency to "chase emotions" is based on the presupposition that we actually have influence over our emotions. Sadly, even though most people frequently "chase emotions", they miss the importance of the fact that they are not the victims of their emotions. We do not have to be the victim of any emotion that the brain can produce! There are things that we do already to change and access certain emotions.

ACTIVITY:

Explore your own strategies for managing your emotions. You already have some experience of changing an emotion from a previous activity. This activity builds on that.

In this exercise, we will deal with your own model for managing two emotional attributes, namely changing content and changing intensity or expressiveness.

You can choose which one you want to work on. But before you start, please note that this is not an appropriate technique for dealing with intense or very negative emotions.

If you choose to work with an experience that started as positive and turned into a negative, please review your selection to ensure that it is not something very important. Alternatively, you might rather want to select something that went from negative to positive.

Think of a time when your initial emotional response to an event changed (for whatever reason.)

Spend a few moments to recall the initial event: like who was involved, what about the event initially caused you to feel the way you did, etc.

Try to recreate it as if you are in the event now.
Which thoughts accompany the feeling, and how are you experiencing the emotion? For instance, where in your body do you feel the emotion?
Does the emotion have a feeling of weight to it (does it feel light or heavy)?
Does the feeling have a shape, and if so, what shape? Where in your chest are you breathing now?
(Please feel free to use any of the other attributes described in chapter 2 to enhance this exercise).

Now, shift your attention to the time when the emotion changed or was starting to change.

What is different now in how you are experiencing and thinking about it? Pay careful attention to how the change started.

However the change started, pay close attention to what your internal experience of it is.

Where did the change in you start?

Did something initiate a new or different way of thinking and then your emotions followed?

Did you become aware of a shift in your emotions first and then only discovered the change in the content of your thinking?

Can you identify a particular pattern or path in this change of your experience?

(This pattern would correspond to your point of change, and a way of tracing it is to pay attention to the sequence of internal events from the beginning until the time when the new experience, i.e. the thoughts and feelings, occupied your attention. If you are comfortable to make fine emotional distinctions, you could also trace the sequence of how you move from any one modality to another, for instance, from pictures to sounds or Kinesthetic experiences).

Questions to help you identify your own model:

a) Which specific issues initiated the change for you? Compare this with at least one other similar event – the commonalities will be used as key factors in your change model.

b) Which values are important to you in this event? What criterion is now being met that was not met before? What was added to your experience that facilitated your new assessment of the situation?

c) Knowing what your change pattern is, and specifically the important "has to happen for me" issues, how can you deliberately apply this for yourself? Now try it out for a "safe" event that you are not comfortable with, and then, before accepting the change, do a thorough ecology check against you highest values.

d) Have you identified the kind of emotion that you can apply your technique to, and under which circumstances it would be appropriate for you to do so? If not, take the time now to do this final step and enjoy the sense of accomplishment that goes with it.

ACTIVITY:

Please think of an occasion in which you made the decision not to express the emotion that you were experiencing at the time. For this exercise, it does not matter if it was a positive or negative emotion. Just as you did in the preceding exercise, notice which thoughts and internal behaviour were instrumental in providing you with the choice. If you need to do this more slowly, here are some questions to walk you through this exercise:

Think of the event and identify some of the characteristics, like:

Who was involved?

What was important to you in that event?

What were you paying attention to?

What was significant about the event?

The decision not to express your emotion could have happened very rapidly, or slowly enough for you to trace the steps, or could have caused an instantaneous halt where the homework happened outside of the event. Let us take one technique at a time.

The traceable response:

The first step: From the moment that you became aware of the emotion, what did you do internally?

- Was your first step talking to yourself, like giving yourself an instruction? If so, what did you actually say to yourself?
- What tone of voice did you use?
- Was it fast or slow?

If the first step was a Kinesthetic awareness, what specifically were you aware of in your body?

The second step: what specifically did you pay attention to next? Pictures? Sounds? Kinesthetics?

The third step? And the fourth? Etc.

The second last step, which is the ecology check.

Lastly, decide in which types of situations this would be an appropriate technique to use, and which emotions you would want to express or not. What would help you to remember when to remember?

These exercises are examples of what we often do without even realising it at the time. But this is the essence of emotional self-mastery.

Congratulations! You have made another exciting discovery of who you are - just say it internally or out loud.

The rapid response:

Whatever point in the process you became aware, that is the place from where you start to trace the sequence. (For the purpose of your own learning, this point of first awareness is also where you should then start the simulation of your success model.)

The interruption pattern:
Even if you did decide to do your homework outside of the event, which of the two strategies did you follow in the event? Then use the appropriate steps above and identify your technique for controlling the expression of an emotion.
You will now have learnt more about what your own internal strategies are for deciding not to express an emotion.

A conclusion: The choice of what to do with an emotion starts with message of the emotion enables you to decide what to do with it: change the emotion and its message, express or withhold the emotion, or reduce the intensity of the emotion.

CHAPTER 4

WORKING WITH YOUR EMOTIONS

Preconditions for Change

The rules in the brain for dealing with behavioural and emotional change
There is a widespread belief that the only way you can get rid of an emotional hurt is to re-experience the pain. In order for you to do that, you have to recall the event – relive it as if it is happening to you in the here and now, and to be completely associated in the experience.

I contend that this is erroneous thinking and the theory above is a total fallacy. In the following section I will put forward an alternative viewpoint that also demonstrates that the ability to dissociate has strong merit not only for emotional self-protection, but also for emotional learning to happen in a rapid, safe and effective way. I will do this in a sequence of safe activities so that we can maintain an experience-based exploration and you can come to your own informed conclusion.

ACTIVITY:

Think of a time when you made an important discovery about yourself, other people, or the world. You may have done this as the result of talking to somebody, or you might have read a book, or something else may have spurred you to do some serious introspection.

As you think about that event, identify for yourself what about the information at the time made such an impact on you that you learned from it. In other words, what are your personal criteria for learning something that you are prepared to act on, as opposed to learning something that is merely "interesting"?

Some learning seems to happen virtually instantaneously. It is possible that there was an unconscious information-gathering process, and the moment of "breakthrough" happens when all the components for believing the new information are in place. It is the tipping point when the person is convinced that the information is true, believable and credible (or whatever the person's criteria for information are in that particular context).

Each step in the process – to be satisfied that the information can be acted on, or that it can be made your own, or is true from a dissociated perspective – is in a sense a different experiential context and the criteria for when you can be convinced will differ in each.

Other learning seems to take much longer, but you may already suspect why this is so, namely because both the information-gathering process as well as what you need to be convinced, are more conscious and more elaborate. Subsequently, these two aspects of the process require much more time.

Learning that takes place over a longer period is, however, not necessarily different in quality (better or more thorough); the length of the learning period may simply be a reflection of the process. Therefore, there is no reason why you cannot learn important information very rapidly, safely and painlessly.

ACTIVITY:

Explore how useful it is to learn from a dissociated position. Think of something in your behaviour that you would like to change, and have told yourself at least once before to stop that particular behaviour, but have not been successful. (Since this activity is, at this stage, just for demonstration purposes, I advise that you do not yet take a serious issue or intense pattern, like stopping smoking or losing weight, until you are more comfortable with the process.)

Step 1: Find a specific example of a situation in which you want to have more behavioural options available.

Step 2: Imagine the behaviour you want to change. It is a bonus if you can pinpoint what specifically it is that you want to change. Now, replay the situation in your mind, but this time, imagine the way you would like to behave. You may even do several iterations until you find the version you like best. (If the novelty of the new behaviour makes you wonder if you can do this, just put those thoughts and doubts in the back of your mind for the time being.)

Step 3: If you acted according to the behavioural option that you have selected, what would you look like, what would your voice sound like, and what feeling would you be aware of as you act in that manner? Please make any adjustments necessary so that it would meet your criteria, and you feel happy with the new behaviour.

Step 4: If you did this behaviour in the identified context, will the behaviour meet with your important criteria? Would there be a price for you to pay? Would there be a price to pay for the other people in the situation? If your answer is yes to any of the last two questions, please go back and make the appropriate changes to your behaviour so that you can say no to all of these questions.

Step 5: Here you have two ways of becoming associated with the new behaviour and make the change your own. One way is to "step into" the behavioural version that you have just planned. A second way is to "put it on" like a shirt and allow it to fit you perfectly.

Step 6: To help you to remember this new behavioural choice when you need to implement it in future situations, think of something that could act as a reminder for you to trigger the chosen behaviour when needed. It could be a person's face, or their voice, or the first inklings of the feeling that you experience in the situation. Having identified the cue to remind you, mentally rehearse the connection until you experience the link as happening spontaneously. Here is how: Think of the cue that will remind you, and the moment you think of the cue, switch your attention immediately and very rapidly to the behaviour you intend to do, as if you were actually doing the behaviour right now. Stop.

Repeat the cycle: cue to the behaviour and stop. Do this another two to three times until your experience it as happening by itself.

Please congratulate yourself for utilising a natural process in the mind to do a piece of change work in a safe and painless manner.

Let's explore some general rules for change, including ways of changing and controlling your emotions.

Mind processes have a positive intention

At the risk of oversimplifying, one can state that the mind has two functions, firstly to develop optimally and secondly, to protect you from intense, unpleasant sensations (very loosely called "hurt"). Unless these two functions are in an appropriate balance, the person is at risk. For instance, if the mind is inappropriately protective, like in the case of a phobia, the other function of the mind cannot do its "job" properly, and you are subsequently deprived of a developmental opportunity.

Exploring your capabilities without proper attention to the safeguarding of your criteria can lead to personal and other damage. Therefore, when you hurt, your mind is using a deliberate strategy to protect you from similar experiences. It is also true that the mind can get "over-enthusiastic" in its protection and could overreact and protect even when it is not necessary, or ill-define a situation as the same even when it is not, and still produce the protective response.

Excessive protection in an interpersonal context can, for instance, result in you wanting to have a relationship, but not permitting yourself because you cannot distinguish clearly enough between safety and danger. Therefore, the price you pay is an imbalance of protection and personal development.

An emotion reflects a judgement...

and unless the judgement is changed, the emotion will not "go away"

When you are angry, you are angry because you experience that a criterion of yours has been violated. Unless you change your thinking about the event, the anger stays because the message is still the same. In the same way, severe emotional pain is your mind's response to an event, with all the mind's protective abilities mobilised in your defence. One can even theorise that psychiatric medication can have a long-term positive effect for those people who use the effect the medication has on their emotions to learn some valuable lessons. This learning would involve them thinking differently about their circumstances, and this change in perception and the resultant change in behaviour, would then contribute to emotional change and the success of their treatment.

The brain cannot process a negative

The brain cannot help thinking of that which it is not supposed to think about. Confused? That is probably what your brain experiences when you try "to not do" something in your mind, called the "pink elephant trap". People who routinely break diets often succumb to this pitfall because they drive themselves to failure by developing an obsession for exactly the foods they should not be eating on their diet plan. This is also in evidence when you tell a child not to let the cup they are holding fall on the floor – and of course, by the time you finished your sentence, you have to go and clean the floor around a very embarrassed child.

For the mind to process a negative, it has to go through two steps: firstly, access that which it has to cancel, and then secondly, do the replacement. The only way the mind can deal with "not thinking" is to replace the content with an alternative. The mind cannot think of "nothing", or a negative. "Not" is a construct of language, not an experiential reality. The closest your mind can get to "not" doing is to refrain from acting on the reality that you are thinking about. Telling yourself to not be afraid is insufficient information for your mind. Only when you give yourself an alternative to being afraid are you actually speaking the language of the brain.

I am sure you have had the experience of wanting to change your behaviour in a certain situation, and undertake not to do it again, only to fail or be disappointed? I suggest it is because you did not complete the process by giving your mind the "instead of" (see the previous activity for a useful procedure for self-change).

Briefly, the same rules apply to emotional change: trying to stop an emotion is looking for trouble; it is like shooting the messenger. The question should rather be "how do I want to feel instead of..." To change an emotion, you have to change how you think about and judge an event. This possibility is also indicative of the reciprocal relationship between thought processes and emotions. In the chapters that describe the interventions, you will notice that one can facilitate change at one of two points in the process: the thoughts or the emotions. If the one way of being helpful does not work, you can just try another way.

More specifically, here are four pointers for personal change:

State your outcome in the positive

It is best to give your mind a positive model as an endpoint.

Desiring not to feel a certain emotion is not sufficient help.

Typical thinking here would be to think about the "best" emotion for you to have in that particular context, that is, the emotion that would allow you to think and behave in a way that would meet your highest criteria for yourself.

To summarise:

- Firstly, what do I want to feel in the place of the emotion I am experiencing?
- Secondly, what specific emotion, if I experienced it, would enable me to meet my highest criteria for that context?

The "instead of" emotion should be something that you can initiate and maintain

Since you are dealing here with your own experience and judgement, it is appropriate to think about how you would want to think and feel about the event. If the starting point of this change in thinking is outside of you, you make yourself dependent on that source to "change your mind". It does not matter whether it corresponds with the opinions of other people in your life; only your opinion matters.

If this is a novel concept for you, please return to the activity on criteria and start by eliciting your own criteria for the context. This will be your starting point to establish what would be important to you and which feeling would support your thinking.

The language of the brain

To supply the brain with a positive model for an outcome, you need to go beyond the level of mere language and present the alternative in the way the brain experiences or "codes" content. In other words, you need to address your brain in its language, in a way that is compatible with how it codes experience. The language of the brain is the pictures, sounds and feelings you pay attention to in your mind.

An important aside: even though I am speaking the language of the senses, what I am referring to here is the data from the senses after it has been processed. This means that once the sensory data have been organised through the filters in your mind at that incredibly fast rate, your experience of the experiential data is not sensory data anymore. The content of the pictures, sounds and feelings are now your very private experience or "coding" of that event.

The rules for change are exactly the same: you need to supply your mind with a complete sensory code as a model for the alternative experience. Even though your focus would be on the feelings, thinking about it in a complete sensory mode makes the model of the outcome so much more powerful. Therefore, to think about the alternative, please think of what you would look like, sound like and feel like with this new feeling or mindset. Keep making adjustments until all the components (as an integrated whole) fulfil your criteria of how you would want to be in that situation. If any one of the components does not feel natural to you, make the appropriate adjustments until it feels good and natural, and you get an integrated sense of wholeness.

Next, you have to do an ecology check. To understand this, get ready for the next section.

Ecology check

Whatever changes you consider, the most important step of all is that the outcome is supported by your criteria. Before you consider any change-work to be final, I would strongly urge you to assess the outcome against your highest criteria for the context. Until the alternative that you consider is absolutely compatible with your criteria, this would not be a good change for you and you would have to repeat the change procedure.

One of the ways you would know that the alternative is compatible with your criteria is that when you consider the outcome against your criteria, you will feel good about the change. Any discomfort with the change is most probably a signal that the change does not meet your criteria and is therefore "not ecological".

In some rare cases, you might consider the "price" a worthwhile one for the more serious discomfort of the original situation, and you might choose to go ahead with the change regardless. If this is the case, I suggest that you consider the opinion of a professional or an "objective" person as a sounding board before you finally make the change.

Context matters

A final test for an ecological change is that it is related to and relevant to the context. This refers to the form of the particular emotion that would be relevant and custom-designed for the context.

Have you noticed that it is as if you have different versions of the "same emotion"? It is easy to explore this concept for yourself: think of two different situations in which you experienced the same emotion and notice the subtle differences both in what the emotion felt like, and your experience of the total event. This will alert you to what I mean with different versions of the same emotion.

The relevancy of this is that you need to verify for yourself that the version of the feeling will be what you would require for the context to achieve your outcome and to meet your criteria for the event. These rules for change apply to everybody because they are the rules by which the brain processes experience.

Logical Levels of Experience and Functioning

One possible, and powerful, way to understand the messages of your emotions is to consider the logical levels which Robert Dilts has formulated and is now using in his Success Factor Modelling. (If you need to know more about the logical levels, I can recommend the extensive material available on the website www.nlpu.org). Each level has its own "logic" or set rules and conditions. Your emotional message may refer to any of the levels. Typically, the higher level influences the content of the lower levels. For example: if I define myself as a curious person, then my values and beliefs, my competencies, my behaviour and the environments I like to expose myself to will reflect my identity. If it does not, I will experience "cognitive dissonance" or feel out of sorts with myself. In this regard I am also relying heavily on Kate Burton's work, especially NLP for Dummies, which provides an excellent overview and practical applications.

> **ACTIVITY:**
> 1. Think of a time when you did something which really made you feel proud and true to yourself.
>   Or, think of a time when you realised how you have changed for the better.
> 2. Unpack that experience using these questions I have compiled from my own work, as well as that of Robert Dilts and Kate Burton. Select the question under each heading that works best for you. The other questions are just options to get your mind going.

Purpose: "This 'beyond-identity' level connects you to the larger picture when you begin to question your own purpose, ethics, mission, or meaning in life. Purpose takes individuals into the realms of spirituality and their connection with a bigger order of things in the universe, and it leads organisations to define their raison d'être, vision, and mission. Human survival amid incredible suffering, depends on true acceptance of your circumstances that goes beyond identity. Witness the resilience of the Dalai Lama driven from his homeland of Tibet, or the story of Viktor Frankl's endurance of the Holocaust in his book Man's Search for Meaning. As you become older and approach different life stages, you quite naturally start to question what you are doing with your life. Sometimes a trigger inspires action and lights up your passion." (from Kate Buron's NLP for Dummies)

This comparison might come in many varied shapes, like the person comparing themselves to a time when their religious life met with their own standards, which it now does not. It might be that they have done something that they feel they should not have done because they should have known better. They could be comparing themselves with a person who is spiritually advanced and dedicated, and feel hopeless to achieve that level of development. Please remain aware – especially in the area of religion – of not becoming too helpful too soon, as this would deprive them of the opportunity to develop as a person.

> **Questions:**
> What was your purpose in starting this process?
> What was your intended outcome?
> What have you realised in achieving this outcome?
> If you were trying to make a contribution to others: what was it? Why that?

Identity: The essence of identity statements is that they are statements of who a person is in a particular context. They reflect your role definitions or role flexibility across different situations/contexts. For instance, you fulfil X-number of roles on any given day, from multiple roles in your career, to variations of roles with regards to your family when you get home. In each context you are a slightly different version of you that collectively make up who you are. This implies that a way to functionally think about yourself is to consider that your name is the name of a collection. A useful analogy to employ is to think of yourself as a museum with different sections and, depending on the interests of the visitors, people would visit, explore and get to know different kinds of art.

Typical statements that one would hear concerning comparisons about a person's identity are:
> "I have lost my true self in the process of ___________."
> "I have become the kind of person I do not want to be."
> "I do not know who I truly am. Who am I really?"

"I wish I could be like _ they are so ______, they seem to be _______, etc."

The strategy for identity statements is to pinpoint the definition with the appropriate specificity for the context, so that the person can fulfil the well-formed conditions of an outcome for the definition of how they would want to experience themselves in a particular context.

Questions:
What kind of person are you when you think back on yourself in this situation?
How would you describe yourself in the situation you are thinking about?
Thinking about yourself, what would you look like, sound like and feel like in the situation you are thinking about?
What would other people say about you in this situation?
Would other people think of you as would like them to?
In what way is what you are experiencing an expression of who you are?

Values: These are the criteria against which the person makes judgements. These judgements are applied to all areas of life and are typically exclusive, like the rightness or wrongness, goodness or badness, effectiveness or non-effectiveness, etc. of an action, experience or event. It takes deliberate discipline for the mind to suspend a judgement for a time – or not to make one. (See Chapter 1 on the rapid and unconscious nature of value judgements.)
The values of a person who is spiritually active – the values they use to make comparisons and judge the world with – are defined by, and derived from, their religion. The source of your conscience is in the self-judgement you make concerning your collection of values. An interesting aside is that some cultures have a guilt-orientation that they use as their internal representation of their values as the basis on which to judge. This judgement is done by self and is a private affair: self judges self on behalf of the community whose values they have internalised.

Other nations have a shame-orientation as their way of monitoring their own right or wrong behaviour in reference to other people: being caught out is where the embarrassment lies. Until you are caught out and "lose face", i.e. become ashamed, behaviours are good; being caught out is bad. Their way of monitoring their behaviour is through, and with reference to, other people: others judge self on behalf of the community. Either way, the outcome of the comparison, when judged "not good", can lead to the painful experience called sadness or depression.

Questions:
What factors are important to you in this situation?
What are you paying attention to in this situation?
What do you believe to be right and wrong in this situation?
How did this situation come about?
When do you say "must", "should", "must not", and "should not"? What assumptions lie behind these statements about what is possible?
If this situation is the effect, what do you believe is the cause?

Beliefs: These are musings about what makes things the way they are. It is the person's way of understanding and/or explaining the world they live in and experience. Beliefs are not always formed consciously and, in a sense, form part of the cultural legacy we inherit as we grow up.

The way we learn to understand the world seldom gets updated, and we can die with a very naive way of thinking and never find a reason to review our initial definition of the world and its phenomena. (Howard Gardner describes the relevant research in his book, The Unschooled Mind.)

In fact, people often vehemently defend their view of what makes the world go round, as if what they know is more valid than expert opinion. It is noteworthy that experts in a particular field, or people who make a career in a particular area, only update their view of their "world of work", but maintain their basic beliefs regarding the world in general.

It can be a very disconcerting experience to discover that your basic view of the world is not valid, and that you have to update your understanding.
This experience of a "lost world" (the world as you knew it), can leave people with a sense of a gap in their understanding of the world. Simultaneously, this "new" world has now also become threatening in its demand for a "new" understanding.
Mourning for the way things were will express itself as sadness or depression.

Competencies: These are the mental processes that you "run" when you do your thinking. These are the things we normally refer to as skills, attributes or abilities.
If the judgement is that the person is under-utilising their abilities, this discrepancy with what they know they are capable of becomes the source of a hurt.

Questions:
What skills or competencies must you have had to have been able to do this?
What part of your competency or skills set came as a surprise to you and would you like to remember?

What do you think others will say if you ask them which competencies   they think you have demonstrated?

What is next? What more would you like to learn?

Behaviour: External behaviour flows from internal mental processes. This comparison comes into play when, for instance, a person stopped doing certain behavioural things that they considered valuable. Coming to that realisation, with the resultant experience of loss for the benefit they used to get, is the source of their sadness.

Questions:

What kinds of behaviour did you display to get to your goal?

How did you decide on those types of behaviour?

How do you know whether those types of behaviour actually helped you to reach your goal?

Do you talk to yourself? What do you find yourself habitually saying to yourself?

How did your breathing change, and when?

What body language did you adopt in this situation?

Environment/Context: The details of when, where and with whom experiences happen. Situations are compared in terms of what experiences are being had and its relevance to the person's identity and values. If it supports the identity and values, then it is experienced as a good situation. If it detracts from the person's wellbeing with regard to their identity or values, this experiential gap is experienced as sadness. (See above: Comparing an ongoing experience with what could/should be).

Questions:

When and where did you achieve this success?

Was it in more than one context? And if so, how were they related, if at all?

Who was involved? Who was part of your "environment"?

What kind of people did you like to have around you?

Who were involved and how did they help or hinder the achievement of your goal?

What did you learn from this regarding other people's support?

At this point, you should have information both about the context and the message and can proceed with the technique for changing the emotional content as described in detail in Chapter 7.

Remember to be respectfully helpful.

Logical Levels

One powerful way to possible way understand messages of your emotions is to consider the logical levels which Robert Dilts has formulated (and now doing extensive great work using it in his Success Factor Modelling). If you need to know more about the logical levels the website NLP.org is rich, as well as Kate Burton's book (see Further Reading at end of the book). Each level has its own "logic" or set rules and conditions. Your emotional message may refer to any of the levels. Typically, the higher level influences the content of the lower levels. For example: if I define myself as a curious person, then my values and beliefs, my competencies, my behaviour and the environments I like to expose myself to will reflect my identity. If it does not, I will experience "cognitive dissonance" or feel out of sorts with myself. I am relying heavily on Kate Burton's material. For detail and the original please refer to her book "NLP for Dummies" an excellent overview and practical.

> **Activity:**
> Thnk of a time when you did something which really made you feel true to self and proud. Or, a time when you realised how you have changed for the better.
> Unpack that experience using these questions from Robert Dilts, Kate Burton and me. Select the question under each heading that works best for you. The other questions are just options to get your mind going.

Purpose

"This 'beyond–identity' level connects you to the larger picture when you begin to question your own purpose, ethics, mission, or meaning in life. Purpose takes individuals into the realms of spirituality and their connection with a bigger order of things in the universe, and it leads organisations to define their raison d'être, vision, and mission. Human survival amid incredible suffering depends on true acceptance of your circumstances that goes beyond identity. Witness the resilience of the Dalai Lama driven from his homeland of Tibet, or the story of Viktor Frankl's endurance of the Holocaust in his book Man's Search for Meaning. As you become older and approach different life stages, you quite naturally start to question what you are doing with your life. Sometimes a trigger inspires action and lights up your passion. " (from Kate Buron's "NLP for Dummies")

> **Questions:**
> What was your purpose for starting on this outcome?
> What was your intended outcome?
> What have you realised in achieving this outcome?

If you had a contribution to others in mind: what was it? Why that?

Identity:

The essence of identity statements is that they are statements of who a person is in a context. They reflect your role definitions or role flexibility across different situations/contexts.

Questions:

What kind of person are you when you consider you in this situation?
How would you describe yourself in the situation you are thinking about?
Thinking about yourself, what would you look like, sound like and feel like in the   situation your are thinking about?
Imagine, what would other people say about you in this situation?
Would other people think of you as you want?
How is what you are experiencing an expression of who you are?

Values and Beliefs:

These are the criteria against which the person makes judgments. These judgments are applied to all areas of life and are typically exclusive, like the rightness or wrongness, goodness or badness, effectiveness or non-effectiveness, etc. of an action, experience or event.

Questions:

What factors are important to you in this situation?
What are you paying attention to in this situation?
What do you believe to be right and wrong in this situation?
How did this situation come about.
When do you say 'must', 'should', 'must not', and 'should not'? What assumptions lie behind these statements about what is possible?
If this situation is the effect, what do you believe is the cause?
What are your convictions about this person or situation? Are these convictions helpful or hindering? What is another way of thinking that is more helpful?

Competencies:

These are the mental processes that you "run" when you do your thinking. These are the things we normally refer to as skills, attributes or abilities. If the judgment is that the person is underutilizing their abilities, this discrepancy with what they know they are capable of becomes the source of a hurt.

Questions:

What skills or competencies must you have to have been able to do this?

What about your competency skill set is a surprise, that you would like to remember?

What may you hear if you ask others to say what they think which competencies   have you demonstrated?

What next? What would you like to learn?

Behaviours:

External behaviour flows from internal mental processes. This comparison comes into play when, for instance, a person stopped doing certain behavioural things that they considered valuable. Coming to that realization, with the resultant experience of loss for the benefit they used to get, is the source of their sadness.

Questions:

What behaviours did you do to get to your goal?

How did you decide on those behaviours?

How did you know those behaviours were being helpful to reach your goal?

Do you talk to yourself? What do you find yourself saying habitually?

How did your breathing change, and when?

What body language did you adopt in this situation?

Environment:

The details of when, where and with whom experiences happen. Situations are compared in terms of what experiences are being had and its relevance to the person's identity and values. If it supports the identity and values, then it is experienced as a good situation. If it detracts from the person's wellbeing with regard to their identity or values, this experiential gap is experienced as sadness. (See above: Comparing an ongoing experience with what could/should be).

Questions:

Where did you achieve this success? More than one context? How were they related, if at all

Who was involved? Who was part of your "environment"?

What kind of people did you like to have around you?

Who were involved and how did they help or hinder your goal achievement?

What   are you learning from this regarding the support of other people?

Congratulations! You have made another exciting discovery of who you are.

In conclusion: Information alone is a poor change agent and somewhat of a hit-or-miss way of making change happen. This is why people can spend years in psychotherapy with questionable success, because unless and until the insight is translated into "the language of the brain", it remains mere linguistic information that is about knowing and not about change.

Therefore, the preconditions for change are that the outcome has to be in brain-compatible code, stated in the positive, meets your own criteria (and not the advice-giver's idea of "good or mature"), is context-relevant and specific; and is initiated and maintained by you yourself.

CHAPTER 5

HOW TO BRING ABOUT CHANGE

Mastery – How to do it

One way to change an emotion is to deal with the message itself. In a nutshell, the steps are:

- Agree on the relevant context for which the person needs emotional first aid and give it a name.
- What is significant about this experience?
- Agree on what the message is.

Discuss and agree on an outcome statement, or the alternative experience the person would like to have (with due consideration to the well-formed conditions of an outcome). How differently would the person have to think about the event in order to change the message? Check that the new way of thinking about the event is ecological.

Agree on the relevant context for which the person needs emotional first aid and give it a name.

At this point, it is useful to remember a couple of things covered in previous chapters, namely:

- We are dealing with the "embodiment of meaning", in other words, the feeling part of an experience, which is the message that results from the rapid judgement that is made during an experience.
- One of the key characteristics of experience is that it is context-specific because it is about a particular time, place, and/or person.
- When you ask the person to identify the context and give the experience a name, you are using the language part of the person's experience as a starting point, so be mindful of the fact that the words they use to talk about their experience have very personal, and even private, meanings for them.

Emotions are therefore messages about a person's judgement in a particular experiential context – the "embodiment of meaning".

The first step is to help the person to identify the message of the emotion, i.e. what specifically is the event or experience about? This is an especially important step if the person has already done some reflection about the emotion in an effort to understand the incident, and has started to generalise the meaning of the original event. You can spot a typical generalisation when the person draws a conclusion about a whole category of contexts and their language includes words like all, always, every time, never, etc. When you hear general conclusions, you can use questions like:

- "When was the first time you became aware of this emotion?"
- "What was the first event that made you come to this conclusion?"
- "What situation gave you the idea that this is how things are?"

These questions are a way of helping the person to go back to the original experience, before the generalisation, so that you can pay attention to the message as it was experienced. If the person did not generalise, it nevertheless invites them to remember the starting point for the message.

Having ascertained that you are dealing with a painful, but non-traumatic event (and if you are not sure, stop right here), then you can ask something about the event itself, like when and where it happened, who was involved, or who was with them at the time?

[If the person becomes emotional at this first question, or they indicate it was a serious event, like an accident, or a rape, etc., then you gently stop the discussion. To help them to move away from the emotion, distract them by doing a "break state" (described in Chapter 8 on using movement as a technique for changing an emotion), or by finding a topic of mutual interest that would get them to pay attention to something positive. Then recommend that they go see a licensed therapist.]

By asking some contextual questions, you get the person busy with the original experience so that you can hear the initial judgement, and deal with that, as opposed to dealing with the veritable mountain of subsequent experiences that have been generalised and lumped together. Giving the event a name, like disappointment, anger, hurt, etc., makes it easier for the person who experienced the event, but is also helpful to the listener in two ways:

- Firstly, it gives you a name by which to call the event and use it as an anchor so that the person can stay with one event at a time.
- Secondly, the name is already the first hint of which criteria have been violated.

What is significant about this experience?

From our own experience about life, we all have ideas about what certain experiences mean. When a person shares their experience with us, it improves the quality of the relationship if we really can understand what things mean to them. You have to be very cautious with the deductions you make about their experiences. When listening to them, it is important to stay with their experience as they unfold it and not to be hasty in jumping to conclusions about what you think their experience means. The key here is to ask so that you hear the correct version the first time and work with what the person offers, and not with your map of the event.

I have often been surprised by the answers people gave about what particular events meant to them. These surprises served to remind me that people have very private and personal ways of being in the world. It taught and reminded me that it is not actually the event itself that determines the meaning, but rather how people experience it and the meaning they ascribe to it with their hearts and minds.

Let me share with you some examples from real case studies of mine:

- A man wanted to commit suicide because he lost his job. When I asked him makes losing his job so important that he is considering suicide, his answer was: "I am now less than a man because I cannot provide for my family, and because I cannot do that, they will not respect me anymore. I cannot stand the idea of looking at my son and seeing the scorn in his eyes. That is the reason I want to remove myself." So for him, it wasn't losing his job per se, but his anticipation of his family, and his son, losing respect for him.
- A person was arrested for fraud, and while in custody awaiting trial, made an unsuccessful suicide attempt because "I cannot stand how people I know will laugh at me for getting caught."
- A woman I counselled after she was raped by three people said that the most dreadful part for her was the fear that they would injure her to the point where she cannot have her own children. Her flashbacks were about all the things they had done to her that might have harmed her to such an extent that it would deprive her of a family.

The above examples illustrate that it is not actually the events of losing a job, being arrested for fraud, or even being raped that caused the hurt, but ultimately what these events meant for the people, and in two cases, even lead them to consider suicide. It would have been very easy and natural to blame the event for their hurt, because I can just imagine what it must have been like. But then I would have missed the very personal message the events had for these people.

Interestingly enough, this is also a feature of very fortuitous events. Here is a simple way of testing this idea: Say you just won a vast amount of money, what about having won the money is the "good" news? Ask this question to some other people that you know and be prepared to be pleasantly surprised that anyone would want to do that with money received "on a plate".

Agree on what the message is
Pay attention to the emotion(s) you are experiencing right now, and ask yourself: "if the emotion I am currently experiencing is a message about me, what would I be

saying to myself?" If the emotion you are experiencing is positive, it means that you are presently meeting a criterion that is important to you as you are reading this. If the emotion is negative, it would indicate that one of your criteria is not being met. If, for instance, you felt impatient, and you asked yourself what is the message to yourself, your answer would reflect which criteria are not being met at present. For example, what might be important to you when reading information like this, is that you are given lots of detail, and you are impatient because the information is not meeting your criteria for detail.

In order to elicit the person's message about the event, you can approach them with two questions: The first question is: "If the emotion that you are now aware of is a message to yourself, what would you be saying to yourself with the emotion?"
The other question would be to ask about the criteria relevant to the situation, since your emotions are a reflection of your present set of criteria. Typical questions that give you information about a person's criteria/values are:
- What would you want from or in this situation?
- What is important to you in this situation?
- What are you paying attention to in this situation?
- What is significant to you in this situation?

Having heard the criteria, the emotion shows whether the criteria are being met or not through the positive (being met) or negative (not being met) quality of the emotion. If this is a situation for emotional first aid, then the message will be a negative one and the person is, by implication, asking about an alternative to the original experience.

Since the rules for positive and negative messages are the same, this technique is also a very useful way to get to know yourself better. Here are two ways to make very pleasant discoveries about yourself:

> Make a list of all the different activities that you experience as pleasant, and ask yourself what is the message about yourself?

> If you want to explore who you really are, review all your "feel-good" memories, and it will give you a topographical map of the landscape of who you are.

It is important to pay attention to the particular words people use when they mention their criteria and the emotional message, and in further conversation, make sure you use the name they prefer. Once you have agreed on the word to use for their emotional message about the event under review, you can proceed to the outcome as discussed under the next heading.

Get to an outcome statement, or the alternative experience the person would like to have.
This section is about how to get to the alternative experience the person would like to have (with due consideration of the well-formed conditions of an outcome). How could the person think of the event in a different way in order to change the message?
For an outcome statement to be well-formed, there are four experiential conditions it has to comply with, namely, it has to be stated in the positive, it has to be something that you can initiate and control, it has to be in the "language of the brain", and it has to be perceived as possible.

The idea of the alternative has to be stated in the positive so that the person can provide their brain with a model that it can make real. Stating what you don't want, or what has to stop, is not enough information for the brain to know what to do instead of it. The brain needs a positive model that it can see, hear, feel, smell and taste.

The choice people have in the world is not so much about what will happen to them, but of how to experience and interpret whatever happens to them. When we make available to people some emotional first aid, our concern should be about how they experience the event. The core question here would be about what the part is that they can initiate change for, and be responsible to maintain that change. The short answer is that emotional first aid is, firstly, about your experience of the event and not about things you can do to change the other person or people involved, or about wishing these things had never happened in the first place. Your experience is the part that you can do something about when using the techniques of emotional first aid.

As we discussed in the chapter on "rules for change", one has to think about the alternative in pictures, sounds and feelings for the brain to be able to process the information in a way that it will lead to change. If the message that the person would like to have about the event is not coded as pictures, sounds and feelings, it will merely be regarded as information, without any difference in the actual experience of the event. Knowing, and even understanding, is not nearly enough to initiate change, as people who have gone through months and years of psychotherapy will tell you. Knowing why something is the way it is might be good for understanding, but not nearly enough for knowing how to change. Unless knowledge is translated into the "language of the brain" it cannot lead to new behaviour or a different experience, because it is seen and coded as information at a language level and not as a model that the brain can use for doing or experiencing.

Each of us has our own way of becoming convinced that something is true or possible. Unless the person is convinced that the outcome is a real possibility for them, they will either argue against it, or say that it is not how things work for them. So-called "resistance" is the person's way of saying either that they do not agree, or they are not sure it is possible for them. This is a demand on the helper's flexibility and respect for the other person; the message is not that there is something wrong with the person, but rather that the helper is at fault in missing the person's reality. Resistance in the person is a sign of disrespect on the part of the helper.

Four steps to a well-formed condition for an outcome

1. **What inner experience do you want instead of your current one?**

    This step is an invitation to the person to review the event and learn something from it, which will produce a different message and therefore, result in a more acceptable emotion. The technique that is applicable here is called "reframing". The two kinds of reframing that we will pay attention to are reframing of meaning and context.

    - Reframing meaning is to explore what else the event could mean.

    Here is an example: person A is acutely aware of disappointment that resulted from how he was treated by person B. Person B is a work colleague and the message from person A's emotion is that he was not treated with the appropriate respect.

    To get to an outcome statement, one would explore with person A what else person B's behaviour could mean to him.

    Be aware that this is not an opportunity to do a character assassination on somebody else; the issue is the person's experience of the event. It might, for instance, indicate an opportunity for person A to practise his assertiveness skills, or it might mean that he needs to pay more attention to person B; it might mean that __________, etc.

    - Reframing context is to restrict the meaning to the event in which it occurred.

    It also entails exploring the possibility that other events that seem to be the same, could actually have different meanings. To use the example above of being disappointed, acknowledge that for that specific event the feeling of disappointment is accurate, but not to start thinking that this will be the pattern for all future interactions. In the event that this should happen again, what would person A prefer to do instead of just being left with a sense of disappointment?

It is vitally important that you as the listener allow the person to work out the alternative meaning for themselves, and only offer suggestions of possible other meanings if they really get stuck. Why? Because it is more helpful to teach people how to do it themselves as opposed to creating a dependency under the illusion that you know more about them than they know about themselves. Furthermore, one of the preconditions for a well-formed outcome statement is also that it is something the person should initiate and maintain for themselves, based on the understanding that they are working with the part of the experience that they can control.

2. **What is the evidence of the new message for you?**

How will you know that you are running the new message? (Using a computer analogy: if you "run" your new programme in the event, what will you be aware of?)

This step is aimed at translating step a) into the "language of the brain". Ask the person to imagine that they are at this moment thinking the preferred message, and as they are doing it in the here and now, you ask them the following three questions:

- What will you look like in the event as you are "running" the preferred message?
- What will you sound like as you are experiencing the message you prefer?
- How will you feel with the preferred message?

It is important that you pay close attention to the person as they do the exercise; some people only need to hear the instructions once, whereas others find it more helpful to hear each sentence as they complete the previous step in the exercise.

Being attentive to people as they go through the steps of the exercise reassures them of your helpfulness, but it also keeps you alert to notice any difficulty that they may encounter as they do the work, like when they need to be reminded of the steps in the exercise.

3. **Context reminder:**

For the person doing the exercise to be sure in which different situations the work they are doing now is applicable. Questions that are helpful here are:

With whom do you want to think like this?

When and where do you want to think like this?

4. **Ecology check:**

For people to check for themselves that the preferred message is compatible with their own, highest criteria. Questions that are helpful here are:

- If you make this message applicable in the contexts that you thought of, would there be any price for you to pay?
- Does this message meet with your highest criteria?
- Could there be a price to pay for the other people in the event?
- Does the preferred message meet with your highest criteria for other people?

Future pacing – remembering when you need to remember.

This is the final step in helping the person to make the message available in the event that they have been thinking about. With the previous four steps, you have given them a brain-compatible model of how they want to be in an event. The person's brain is now familiar with both the "what" and the "how". Next, they have to rehearse running their programme at the right time, when they need it. The essence of future pacing is for them to run the new programme very rapidly in the mind, and to create a link between the event and their preferred response to it.

The event now becomes the trigger for their brain to think with the preferred response as opposed to its initial reaction.

Try this for yourself first.

ACTIVITY:

Step 1: Start off by thinking of one of the contexts in which you want to run your preferred programme.

Step 2: The instant that you start to think about the event, immediately switch to experiencing your preferred message, and then think about the event through your preferred message. Stay in this experience a while and notice the difference in your experience.

Step 3: Pay attention to something in your environment for a few moments to "clear your head", and then repeat the process of thinking about the event and immediately switch your attention to your awareness of the preferred message that you will now be running through your head.

Step 4: Repeat step 3 with increasing rapidness until your experience is that the

process runs itself. You will likely only have to do this exercise three to five times before you sense it is in place.

Step 5: Do the same, if you need to, for all or some of the other contexts. You will know when to stop when you have an internal sense that your brain will know what to do when you need it.

What do you do if your preferred outcome doesn't pass the ecology test?

Briefly, there are two options: change the form of the outcome representation, or change the outcome.

Changing the form: Changing the form of the outcome means that you change the way you act during the new programme. Specifically, it means changing the way you appear, or sound like, or the feeling that would go with the outcome, which might not have been appropriate and could have been the reason why the response was not ecologically sound. To address this, go back to step 2 and do another version of the outcome by exploring the effect of changing one component at a time until you are comfortable with the ecology of the response. Say, for example, that your first version for being assertive in a certain situation did not pass the ecology test. To change the form, you started off by checking that the way you looked was non-threatening. If that was not enough to take away the uncomfortable feeling, you might have needed to pay attention to your voice and may have realised that you needed to change the way you sounded. You can then explore different ways of saying assertive things until you know it is ecological, where after you can go ahead with the future pacing.

Changing the outcome: This option follows after you have unsuccessfully experimented with changing the form. Try now to think of an alternative outcome that would better meet the well-formed conditions of an outcome. So simply repeat steps 1 to 5.

In conclusion: This chapter is a balance between the art and science to setting goals for change. The science involves the structured approach. The art, however, comes in how you interact with the person with different questions or even a different process sequence. This book is not enough to give you skills in the art. If you need help or need the process to be explained more explicitly, you may need to consult a qualified NLP-practitioner.

This method for changing emotional messages, as well as thought patterns and behaviour, is the standard NLP way of working. Even experienced NLP-practitioners skip steps, like the future pacing, and then get random results. From a change point of view, this is the heart of the book, and it is worth good study so that you can master it for yourself as well as being helpful to other people.

CHAPTER 6

LISTENING

How to Deal with Other People's Emotions

Listening to other people is both difficult and easy. Good listeners do so because they are interested, and therefore, it is easy to pay attention to what other people are saying. It is challenging to listen actively and with respect to what the other person is saying – and stay with what they are saying.

On a lighter note, one could formulate a listener's oath as: "their message, their whole message, and nothing but their message". That would be a very difficult oath to uphold for most of us – even people who are generally good listeners. This is because the interest that goes with listening frequently has an element of "wanting to be helpful" in the mix. And it is this "wanting to be helpful" component that turns a good listener into a bad one. In the process of wanting to help, they can do two unhelpful things, namely, listen only until they can help (which frequently is sooner rather than later), and/or listen and compare with their own experience so that they help from their own experience (with the predictable sentence that introduces the advice: "what I would do..."), assuming that there is similarity where there might not be.

Another trap for the helpful listener to fall into is to share the "insight" that they have about the person's problem with them. This often takes the form of telling the person what their "real" problem is, like giving them a psychological explanation of what "caused" their problem. Of the traps mentioned, this latter is the most dangerous because with this kind of help hurts can be opened, which can be devastating to the person, and defeats the purpose of being helpful. Merely providing information is the least effective way of helping people to change. If information or insight was all that was needed, you could just recommend your current favourite book and it should do the trick (which of course it does not). The long duration of typical psychotherapy is also an indication that even though people might understand their own problem (after a long period sometimes as well as the therapist), they often stay the same and not change their behaviour or their experience.

The importance of listening long enough
An interesting saying that meant a lot to me when I heard it the first time is: "words are unverified rumours". When people share their experiences, the only medium

they have available are the words they use; and words are just the "shorthand" version of what people typically experience. Responding too soon to people's words means exactly that – you will only respond to their (initial) words, and not necessarily to the experience they are trying to communicate. Which simply means that you are not hearing the message; you are only hearing the "rumours". In order for you to listen respectfully to the message, you would have to wait and listen for the person to tell you which of their criteria is relevant. Listening for the pertinent criteria is not only a sign of being respectful, it is also an essential step in understanding what experience, and message about the experience, the person is really expressing with their words. Unless someone is very skilled in how they verbalise their feelings, expect them to search for the "best" words, often by saying the same thing or describing it in two or more different ways; saying it until it sounds "right" or until the words used are the best approximation of the experience.

An important and necessary part of listening actively is to listen for which parts of the person's experience are not being shared so that you would know which questions to ask. Questions are an essential part of listening. Not listening long enough makes it very difficult to know which questions to ask in order to gather the necessary and appropriate "other" information.

In a nutshell: listening for emotional messages is not just about how long you keep your mouth shut, but how long you soak the person up with your full attention (eyes and ears), to hear "their message, their whole message, and nothing but their message".

Listen to the others person's reality
This is about listening to the other person with respect, hearing "their message, their whole message, and nothing but their message." A criticism that can be levelled against some psychiatrists and psychologists is that they are sometimes be so busy listening from the vantage point of their current favourite theory of human behaviour that they do often not really hear what the person is actually saying; they are only paying attention to whatever corresponds with their theory. Their theory might be more complex than some of the "common sense" theories that go around, but it is no different from non-trained helpers who insist that the person's "real problem is..." and amounts to the same thing. In both cases you are not necessarily dealing with the person's experienced reality, and could, in another context, be considered disrespectful because you are not paying appropriate respect to how the person is presenting their information.

For a person to really use information to effect personal change, the information has to meet at least four criteria (see Chapter 3 on "Rules for Change" for a more extensive discussion), namely: (1) The potential learning should happen while they feel safe from hurt and have a sense of personal mastery; (2) it has to be demonstrably relevant to their very personal reality, in other words, that they should see, hear and feel it in a way that is true to their "map" of their experience; (3) it has to be credible to their experience, in that they have veto right about what the experience "really" means since it is their experience when you are using people's emotional or criteria words back at them (see point 4 below); and (4) it has to contain the solution or the alternative experiential options.

Extensive information and research are available on this topic in the field of adult education and successful academic performance. It is strange that even professional helpers ignore this mass of research and insist that when people are labelled as "a patient", the rules for learning in the brain have disappeared and a new set of rules apply, such as the best way for a person to learn about and heal from emotional hurts, is to hurt again by reliving the same hurt. Learning through reliving hurt, means reliving al the negative components that made it a hurtful experience in the first place, exactly as it was. The one principle in adult learning that is taken for granted, is that people learn best when they see the relevance and they feel empowered to master the new information, which is directly opposite to what is implied when a person has to relive their hurt or are being told what is "really wrong" with them.

Listen to their experience as if it is unique in the history of human life
Listening "as if" the person's experience is unique has more than one merit, the most important of which is that it is the truth. While there may be some common characteristics, people ultimately experience events in ways that are as singular as their thumbprints. Their personal history, values and the hierarchy of those values, all contribute to their unique ways of coding experiences. One of the examples of this is how differently people would interpret the same "objective" data. Collecting eye-witness accounts from bystanders at the scene of an accident, for instance, can be a police officer's nightmare because they can get such diverse versions of the event that it may leave you to wonder if they're even describing the same accident. Any comparisons that match two people's experiences are the exception rather than the rule. We often don't realise this, because the differences become hidden in the words that people use, and how the same words may mask a different experiential reality for different people. The fact that you recognise a word does not mean you can necessarily identify with the experience that goes with the word.

ACTIVITY:
Take a value word that has importance for you and identify a context (a specific time, place and/or person) in which it is applicable for you. From your personal experience, how would you know whether somebody is meeting those criteria? What would they have to do or say that would be evidence enough for you that they are complying with your criteria? For how long or how many times would they have to do that for you to have the reassurance that you can trust them to comply with your criteria for that context? Now, ask somebody you know to give you their evidence or recognition cues for the same criteria in a similar context, and compare the two ways of recognising the values/criteria. Could you have predicted that:
- this is important to them?
- they would recognise it in this way?
- they would need this number of times, or period of time, to be convinced?

The point here is that while people could very well use the same words, they have different ways of recognising them in experience and, correspondingly, behave differently to the reality described by the same words. The remainder of this chapter is about listening to other people's realities and the messages they give about their experience of their reality.

What do words really express?
Words give voice to a person's experience and the values/criteria relevant to that experience. To really appreciate this statement, let me remind you of some of the attributes of your experience so that you can use your own experience as the basis for listening to other people's messages about theirs.

"The map is not the territory."
The words a person use are only a reference to or an approximation of the experience. As indicated above, not only do words sometimes mask aspects of an experience, but they may also diffuse the uniqueness of an experience. The minute you try to find experiential similarities based on language alone, you can fall into the trap of equating them, whereas the similarity might only be in using the same word references which might or might not denote similar experiential information. You would not know until you have also compared experiential data such as pictures, sounds and feelings.
Experiences are context specific.

ACTIVITY:

Think of a word of something interesting that you have done recently. Now, think of
the event as if it was happening to you right now.
Notice how you are thinking about the event. What are you paying attention to?

You are bound to notice at least two things from this exercise:

a) The more you are "inside" your experience, the more you tend to think in pictures, sounds, and/or feelings. You might even notice that you have a particular preference, i.e. to think more in one "form" than the other. For example, when you recalled this experience, you spent more time thinking in, say picture form than you do in sound or feeling form. If you think of another experience altogether, your preference might shift to another form.

b) The information content of an experience is very specific to that particular event. It is inherent in the function of language to generalise with words as if things were the same in experience. Try this with another two or three experiences where you use the same words, and you will notice that every time you think about the experience that goes with the word, you tend to think context specifically. You might even notice that even though the words imply similarity, that not only are the informational contents different, but the criteria or feel of the different events are different. These differences could be because of time and place, because of activity, or because something else was important to you, etc.

There are two important factors to keep in mind when we talk about the context-specific nature of experience: Firstly, during the course of a day, you live through a whole sequence of maps or a range of experiences. Secondly, each map or experience itself is complete and would have its own set of values or criteria built into the experience. Experiences that are referred to with the same words might vary in important ways, as indicated in the previous paragraph. Sometimes we also refer to experiences with the same word, but the applicable hierarchy or priority of criteria would differ, making it a different kind of experience altogether.

Emotional meanings and messages are also context specific.
Just as the criteria are context specific, a person's emotional message is also context specific, even for experiences that might be identified or described with the same words. It stands to reason that each experience would have a distinct message, because each message is a context-specific reflection of the context-specific criteria applicable in a context-specific experience. Having said, be aware that people may already have generalised their own experience and, as a consequence, group together situations which, in terms of experience, do not actually belong together. Thus they

do to their internal experience what a not so good listener would do by not listening appropriately.

What does this mean for listening? It means unless you and the speaker have agreed on the context, you will be guessing at what the person is saying; you will have to rely on the unreliability of words, and could be perceived to be a poor listener. Not knowing what context and message are involved, you could find yourself in a position where whatever you say to the person about what you have just heard, they may deny having said that, or deny having meant that, or say that you do not understand. That is the bad news. Read on for the good news about how to listen for emotional messages.

- Information Gathering: What is the Message that I am listening for?
- Listen for the criteria applicable, one context at a time.
- Ask for the meaning of each message per context.

If you know how to do this, go to the next section of your choice. If not, here is how: (Please note: this is for good, helpful listening, and should not to be used for severe emotional pain or emotions that are the result of a traumatic experience. In that circumstance the approach to information gathering would be very different, and would include teaching the person ways to protect themselves emotionally against the painful effects of the incident under discussion.)

1) Agree on the context under discussion.

When people are emotionally upset, their vocabulary and thought processes reflect their emotions, and they might have some difficulty getting "unstuck" from the intensity and effect of the emotion. They may use a lot of generalisations in an effort to express themselves and may provide poor contextual information. Others might verbalise with a flood of words, while others yet may have lots to say about what they would like to do "with" the emotion. Some people might have difficulty giving voice to their emotion and/or experience in the first place, adding to their own frustration by being angry, withdrawing in frustration, or using nonverbal gestures or movements to at least "do" something.

Talking about who was involved, and where and when the experience happened is a good starting point both for the person relating their experience and for the listener. In other words, gather information about the context. This means that both people can stay with appropriate and relevant components of the experience at any period of time, instead of getting caught up in the momentum of the experience. Context-specific data is the information about the experience, and particularly about how the person experienced it, not just a description of the event. A characteristic of this information is that the words used will reflect the experience directly, meaning that it will have a lot of references to what was seen, heard and felt as various elements of the experience.

Sensory-specific information refers to the words people use when they describe an experience as an ongoing event or as it really happened (what is seen, heard, felt, smelt and/or tasted). The sensory-specific information is also useful to the listener, because by asking for it, you help the person to get back to the original, context-specific experience. Here is how it happens: by asking the person sensory-specific questions (i.e. by asking them to tell you what they saw, heard and felt as it was happening to them), you guide them to recall that type of information by paying attention to it with their minds, and therefore, they will think of their experience in the context-specific way that it happened in the original experience. Caution: this way of listening is not applicable for serious or intensely negative emotional events, which depends upon other methods for information gathering and requires training beyond the scope of this book.

2) Agree on the person's criteria that are relevant in this context.
People verbalise their criteria all the time, but are usually not conscious of it; and listeners typically do not pay attention to it, and therefore do not "hear" it. There are two ways of hearing other people's criteria, namely through listening carefully and enquiring about it. Hearing people's criteria as they utter them spontaneously and continuously requires the listener to remember two things and to use their ears twice as much as their mouth. Here are the two things to remember:

When you are listening for a person's criteria, be sure to get them to talk about the context that is relevant to the criteria that you are curious about. Whenever someone expresses a personal preference or makes a comparison, they are articulating a judgement that can only take place through the criteria and will, therefore, either outright express their criteria, or imply it. If they don't declare their criteria, then a simple question like, "why do you say that?" will get the person to state their criteria for that context to you.

> **ACTIVITY:**
> Agree with a person on a topic or a context for a particular experience, then:
> a) Ask them their personal preferences about _______, and listen to how they spontaneously tell you their values/ criteria, or how easily they verbalise them if, under these circumstances, you ask them "why"?
>
> Again, agree with a person on a topic or a context for a particular experience, then:
> b) Ask them to make a comparison with ____, and notice how the comparison allows you to get them to talk about their criteria for that context.
>
> The more "formal" way is to ask directly about the person's criteria, in which case, there are a few further things to remember:

As you are having the conversation with the person about their criteria, agree very specifically with them about the topic or context for your discussion. If you are going to talk about their criteria for buying something, for instance, be clear about buying "what specifically", because they will most likely have different criteria for buying different items, e.g. a car or an item of clothing.

Keep reminding the person of the context you have agreed upon if, while they are talking about their experience and things that are important to them, they get side tracked. Unless you remain vigilant about this, people can start thinking about other contexts, and subsequently give you criteria that are a mixed bag from different contexts, and you would not know unless they are aware enough to tell you they have changed the context while they were thinking (and people are seldom, if ever, this self-aware). This will leave you with low quality information.

One useful way to remind people about the context under discussion is to repeatedly mention the name of the topic or context as you ask them questions to stimulate them to think about the criteria.

The following six questions are some examples of ways of asking the same thing in different ways because most people respond better to certain questions than others. There is no way to predict which question will work for which person, therefore it is helpful to remember all the suggestions so that you can be flexible enough to assist people to discuss their criteria with you.

1. What is important to you when _______?
2. What do you pay attention to when _______?
3. What is significant to you when (or during) _______?
4. When you _______ what are you evaluating?
5. The important considerations when you are _______?
6. What do you want from/in _______?

People do not use value words randomly

These are words that carry very specific meanings of the person's experience and should, therefore, be respected as their "private property". This means that when you reflect a person's criteria back to them to check your understanding or to continue the discussion, you have to be respectful and use the same words as the person did, and not "translate" them into what your equivalents for those words would be. You could even find that if you do a "translation", that people will either not accept the words you offer, or indicate a reluctance to agree with you, as if they did not say what you are implying they have said – and of course they would be correct, because they did not use your words, they used theirs!

ACTIVITY:
This activity is an opportunity for you to practise using one of the six questions above with the person you are going to engage in a conversation.
Step 1: Agree on a topic or a context for discussing a particular experience and then agree on a name for the experience which you can both use as a shorthand to the experience.
Step 2: Start by asking the person any question from the list. If the question is appropriate for the person, they will summarily answer. If they appear reluctant or do not understand the question, ask another question from your list until they start to answer your questions about criteria.
Step 3: One way of encouraging them to explore their criteria is occasionally to repeat their criteria words to them and ask, "what else"?
Step 4: Notice how people will spontaneously offer between three and five criteria. If you keep pressing for more after this point, they will start to give you more general criteria or words that might not actually be relevant to them personally. When you are dealing with a person's experience and maintain the context specificity, research on values from value questionnaires seems to indicate that people operate from only three to five criteria, and not from extensive mental lists. Should you ask people to select values from a value-questionnaire (and you can explore this for yourself), they tend to pick a posy of value words which might or might not have anything to do with the real criteria that influence their experience. Unless criteria are elicited in a context-specific manner, meaning experientially true, the information is interesting from a purely semantic point of view, but does not necessarily reflect the person's operating criteria.
Step 5: Treat the criteria words the person gives you with respect, as it is from their private experience. And remember that the words they use reflect their reality, and their words therefore represent parts of their experience.

3) Agree on the meaning of the emotion that the person is experiencing in this context.

Because this book is about assisting people to deal with emotional difficulty of a non-traumatic nature, you are now ready to explore the meaning of the event under discussion with the person.

A word of caution though: People who are interested to help, such as the readers of this book, are inclined to help because they think or know that they can make a difference based on what they know from experience, or have learned in other ways about life and other people.

That statement contains both good and bad news. The good news: the intention to help is one of the noblest aspects of the human being; almost every major religion uses saintly examples as a model of the ultimate in being human. The bad news: ironically, the desire to help may contribute to increased insensitivity and disrespect for other peoples' realities, leading, in effect, to the opposite of the helper's good intentions. How? You may ask.

When people approach someone seeking help or advice, they often say something to the effect of "I do not know anymore," or "I am here because you may know something I don't," or even, "you know better". Hearing these words often seduces helpers, including professionals, into exemplifying the bad news: the desire to help and agreeing that you (could or might) know better than they do, sets up the next pitfall, namely that as soon as you think you know what help they need, you stop listening. The minute you hear a word that links with your experience and you can draw a parallel with your own experience, you imagine you have enough information to have an answer to give to the person asking for help.

The rest of the information is not heeded, because what was needed to be known, one thinks, has been established and thus no further information is required. Therefore, further information gathering, i.e. listening, is summarily suspended. So what is the lesson?

"People need to be on guard against short-circuiting the discussion by offering a practical solution too early on." (Goleman: *Emotional Intelligence*, p.142.)

Goleman discusses this in the context of marriage, but the point he makes is equally valid in other contexts of listening to any person (not just the wife in the context of marriage) when the intention is to be helpful: "... it's typically more important to a wife that she feels the husband hears her complaint and empathizes with her feelings about the matter ... she may hear his offering advice as a way of dismissing her feelings as inconsequential." (Goleman: *Emotional Intelligence*, p.142.)

Once you've succumbed to that pitfall, you can easily fall into the next one once you dole out your advice. You find yourself thinking something like, "if they get to the same insight as me, then they can do what I would do". Or at least what you imagine you would do. (And "imagine" is definitely the operative word, because if you're honest, you would acknowledge that knowing does not mean doing.) Being so certain of the answer and the thought that "all they have to do is listen and do", the listener is caught in the pitfall of being disrespectful.

All of the above is not nearly an exhausting account of how "knowing and wanting to be helpful" can become insidious traps for disrespectful behaviour, but the point must be made: the minute you sacrifice respect through the lack of effective listening, you become a less than helpful helper! Until you have "their truth, their whole truth and nothing but their truth" you are (maybe) helping yourself through them, but you cannot be busy with them. The final part to listening to another persons' emotional message in order for you to be helpful is therefore to listen to the other persons experience from their experiential viewpoint, cleanly and completely. Here is how!

Listen to the message in the feelings being expressed and get confirmation of your understanding.

What's the message? The message is what the event means to the person, based on their internal assessment of the experience against their context specific criterium. Since this assessment is the result of a rapid unconscious process the person would not necessarily be aware of the meaning (unless they have done some prior, "objective" thinking about the event.) It is therefore most unusual for the person to volunteer what the event meant, and experience indicates that the person will say this meaning component only if guided there by a question by the listener. This means very simply, unless you ask what the event means to the person, you could be making the wrong "informed" guess.

Are there any messages that only experts would know about? The answer is a yes and a no. "Yes" to the possibility that the expert could know the meaning first because the person might not pay attention to what they are saying, and the listener would therefore hear it first.

The answer is "no" to the (expert) listener knowing what the person could not know themselves. The formulation and popularity of the unconscious mind has created an evil in that information that is presented to a person, if they reject it or plead ignorance of it, is attributed to their unconscious mind. I have even heard people trying to accommodate a professional therapist, offering their own "I don't know, it must be in my unconscious mind"!, instead of just disagreeing. The unconscious mind cannot be any part of one that does not "play" along, and is therefore basically transparent, if the circumstances are safe and emotionally manageable.

4) Using people's emotional or criteria words back at them
When people are sharing information from their experience, their words are true reflections of that experience and are therefore laden with personal meaning. What you pay attention to in your mind selects the vocabulary that you use. This means that the words that people use when they trust you enough to share personally private and experienced information with you, are not selected randomly and part of listening respectfully is to pay attention to the words exactly as they use it. When

you test your understanding of what they have told you about their experience, part of the testing is to say their words back at them, because those words are the best representation of their reality.

> **ACTIVITY:**
> Engage a friend in a discussion about something that is important to them and elicit their criteria (as in the activity above when you were practicing the six criteria questions.) Having elicited all the relevant criteria say it back to them, but...use synonyms, and watch their reaction! They will clearly indicate that they do not agree with your understanding. This is a variation of when people argue about what something means or what the correct word to use is, then end up saying it is a question of "semantics".
> It is more than that! It is a disagreement on defining one's reality. (Remind yourself of the exercise in c) The importance of listening to their experience as if it is unique in the history of human life.)

In conclusion: There is a saying in NLP that words are unverified rumours. When practising your listening skill, this is a very apt reminder: hear the person's own words, ask for examples and stay away from assuming that because you recognise the word, you naturally know the map or experience it refers to. Words, when it comes to experience, are unique and personal. Listen as if it is the first time you hear the words.

CHAPTER 7

SADNESS

Or the Missing Piece

One of the most disrespectful things a person can hear when they are sad is: "Stop feeling sorry for yourself!" Disrespectful? Yes! Because what the person is experiencing is exactly that, namely feeling sorry for themselves. They are mourning the absence of something in their lives.

Sadness or depression has a central message that is the result of a very interesting and complex process of judgement. This process of judgement is based on one of the key mental processes in the brain, namely the process of comparison. The message is reflecting the comparison between the everyday self and the best examples stored in memory, with the conclusion that the person is "not doing well". This comparison indicates that the person is operating at below their own internal standards or expectations of themselves. The comparison might equally be a reflection of their assessment of the situation they are experiencing, namely being disappointed with the situation. Specifically, that the event is not meeting their expectations of what they would like to experience. It may even reflect "the meaning of life" question that is not answered to their own satisfaction.

Comparing self with self

Sadness, reflecting the hurt from the judgement of yourself as being less compared to what you are capable of, is based on some powerful, but taken-for-granted information about ourselves:

a) We store everything that has ever happened to us in our memory.
   The key question about memory is not about input, but about retrieving what is already stored.
   This is why, for instance, study methods for students focus on how to input the information with the aim to able to access it on demand. The assumption is that the way of inputting can be helpful to the retrieval of the information. These study methods mostly focus on teaching the candidate different methods for retrieving the information under certain conditions, like exams at school or tertiary institutions.
   Significant experiences are coded in a manner that makes the accessing easier. That ease has to do with the cues used to "find" the information in the data banks of this magnificent supercomputer called the human brain. Significant experiences can be "searched" for in a variety of ways. The basic

mechanism in the search would be comparisons or similarities: the mind would "go find" the information based on what is similar to the cue that the person associates with the particular experience:

- The learning is summarised in your own preferred language/words;
- Key features of the event, like when, where or with whom it happened;
- The feelings that represent the learning;
- The conclusion that you said to yourself;
- What the experience looks like or what the significant thing was that you saw;
- What convinced you that the learning is true?
- Was the information relevant to your identity?
- Was the information from the experience relevant to your values?
- Is it contributing to information about your competencies?
- Was it learning about your behavioural options?

It seems, however, that the mind is more comfortable to generalise the cues for bad news than it is to generalise the cues for good news. Have you noticed how it is easier for people to believe bad news and find evidence for it a lot easier than they do for good news? This would explain why people, in some circumstances, find it easier to find instances of failing and have difficulty to find examples of being successful or smart. (For more about the inclination to believe bad news sooner than good news, read the chapter on trauma, chapter 5, specifically on how people can generalise their thinking after experiencing trauma.)

b) If the brain has done something once, the question then becomes, how do you repeat the performance?
The best exemplars of your capabilities only occur because your brain already has the circuitry. You would not be able to perform something optimally if you (your brain) were not capable of doing it. Unless you have the neuro-circuitry for a particular neuro-action, that action cannot be taken. The challenge then becomes to access the neuro-software on demand, instead of randomly, even for complex strategies like creativity, innovative thinking, excellent problem solving, etc. People who have poor self-image tend to complicate the repeatability of their own successes because they tend to deny ownership of them. "If it's not yours, you can't get it back."

c) Not acknowledging or paying attention to your own successes makes it very difficult to duplicate them.

The successes themselves contain the formula or recipe for future iterations. Your success is a demonstration of the appropriate neuro-software for that particular success in that particular form. Like a computer programme, it has its own code or design in how you think, feel and behave. In order for you to reproduce that success or experience, you need to repeat that code or formula of thinking, feeling and behaving. You can therefore say that repeating your success happens by design and not by chance. Equally, you fail by design too. If you do not repeat your own success formula in a similar event to recall that specific "success programme" when it is ecological to do so, you will not be able to produce the same success. If you want to track your own successes, you may find it helpful to read chapter 3 on the rules for change, because the same principles of the language of the brain apply to reproducing success.

d) The best examples of what you are capable of become the standard for your everyday behaviour.

Even though it might sometimes be difficult to consciously access information about how smart you have been in certain events, the brain does not forget, and uses these known examples as criteria for what you are capable of. These "best examples" are actual experiences and not to be confused by the search for a mythological "ideal self". In other words, this is a real, live, actual example of your own behaviour and experience. In the process of living your daily life, you think and do things that you consider to be appropriate for the events that you encounter. When your response to these events is not a decision for the best that you are capable of, this discrepancy between how you thought and did, as compared with the best you are capable of, is experienced as a discomfort. This, in some people, is experienced as sadness or depression.

If this discrepancy is a matter of values, this discomfort comes as a "message from your conscience", and some people will experience this as sadness about the transgression. In a nutshell, the judgement that you are not doing the best you know you are capable of is, for some people, an experience for which they feel sorry for themselves. They mourn for themselves because they are so aware of the difference between their present state/behaviour and what they are capable of.

Comparing an ongoing experience with what could/should be

Comparing an ongoing experience with what could/should be can be as destructive as comparing yourself with other people. Experiences just are. Other people are who they are; they even have their own names to stake their claim to their unique identity. When comparing an experience or yourself with another person, your intention determines whether this is beneficial or detrimental. If it is about becoming "like that", you are looking for trouble. If, however, it is about learning and enrichment, or personal development, it could be very positive.

There is not a nation in the world that does not have some form of religion. Human beings seem to be "wired" for meaning – and will go to great intellectual lengths to find it. The importance of meaning in people's lives can be seen in the negative effect it has on people if meaning is lost (and they feel their lives are meaningless) or if the meaning is extremely unacceptable – so extreme, in fact, that they will consider suicide to stop the experience. Ascribing meaning is an unstoppable process and experience in the human brain (see chapter 1). A person dealing with these negative effects has all the reason in human existence to mourn and feel sorry for themselves. There is, for them, a significant gap in their experience of events, and one could even say of life itself.

The intensely negative message in this experience is one of stating the absence of an essential component of life. Any experience that reflects a lack of the three S's, namely self-worth, significance and/or security is an alienating experience for any being human, and forms the neurological basis for the imperative to be "fixed". How could one be surprised that people commit suicide, not for the events as described by research, but for the meaning they give those events? It is not the lack of money, or long-term stress, or being caught out in a crime, or failing an exam, etc. that is the root cause of suicide, but what these events mean to the person. Furthermore, these events have such an intensely negative meaning that they consider death to be a better choice over the meaning that is being experienced. Once people have made this decision, it becomes very difficult to prevent them from committing suicide. Treating how they feel is not enough, because the feeling is just the messenger, and as long as the message is valid, the feeling will stay.

(Notice how defining a depression as biological not only destroys the beneficial effects of hope and optimism, but removes the underlying sense of "efficacy" as well.)
One of the main determinants of whether a depressed mood will lift or persist is the degree to which people ruminate. "Depressed people sometimes justify this kind of rumination by saying that they are trying to "understand themselves better"; in fact, they are priming the feelings of sadness without taking any steps that might actually lift their mood. Thus in therapy it might be perfectly helpful to reflect on the causes

of a depression, if that leads to insights or actions that will change the conditions that cause it. But a passive immersion in the sadness simply makes it worse." (Goleman, p. 71). "As Wenzlaff told me, thoughts are associated in the mind not just by content, but by mood. People have what amounts to a set of bad-mood thoughts that come to mind more readily when they are feeling down…" (Goleman, p72.)

Mood lifters

These are immediate, but short-term mood-changing first aid methods that one can use. However, they are exactly that: immediate, short-term techniques for lifting a person's mood.

1. **While crying can sometimes break a spell of sadness, it can also leave the person still obsessing about the reasons for the despair.** Crying that reinforces the rumination only prolongs the misery. Talking about the sadness is helpful if it takes place in the proposed format of changing the message and taking responsibility for making a new message valid. (See below: changing the message.)

2. **Distractions can be very helpful as it invites the person to pay attention to something else.** You could cheer yourself up, for example, with treats and sensual pleasures. Shifting your attention to something else occupies the brain with other content and other processes, and if it continues for long enough, you will notice a shift in your feeling state that will be more indicative of this new preoccupation of the mind.

   Clinical experience indicates that the most effective distractions are the ones that will shift your mood. The effectiveness of this technique depends on the extent to which you can immerse yourself in, or keep yourself occupied with, whatever the distraction is. If people are too depressed, they will have difficulty switching their attention sufficiently to the distraction, because their emotions act as an anchor that keeps their thoughts in line with the emotions. It is this anchoring effect of emotions – especially that of severe depression – that makes people in their immediate vicinity very impatient because they cannot understand why the person does not "snap out of it".

   In the case of longstanding depression and stress, the person's physiology changes as a way of coping with the "emotional coding", and this physiological pattern further enhances the anchoring effect of the emotions. This anchoring effect is frequently, and erroneously, explained as "endogenous depression" when, strictly speaking, the clinical profile of the person does not match that of genuine endogenous depression.

3. **Exercise, because it helps to change your physiology**. (Refer to chapter 8 for more information and the brain gym activities to shift an emotion.)

4. **Engineer small triumphs or easy successes, and pay attention to the kinesthetic difference**. This is a very powerful strategy because people who are caught up in their own judgement of "not enough", sometimes give up hope of any success, or forget how to feel successful. This mood-lifting technique is a way of getting them to remember good feelings, as well as giving them a model for how it is possible to "create" positive emotions.

   The type and grading of these activities are important, since the outcome should be an experience of success for the person. Be careful, therefore, that the activities agreed to with the person are guaranteed to lead to an experience of success.
   For starters, rather focus on the frequency rather than the magnitude of the successes. This means very simply that the activities should be manageable and lead to certain success in a particular time cycle, for example, in the course of a day or just a few days.

5. **Success is the key, so the activities can initially be simple and mundane rather than starting off with something that will take major mental effort and complex, abstract thinking**. It is about starting with the new mindset and getting used to, and comfortable with, closing the gap that is currently the source of the sadness. Do not expect to be bowled over by the person's enthusiasm, especially if the sadness has a history, or if the person is already convinced that they suffer from "biological depression". (A word of caution: there is a small percentage of depression that is clinically endogenous. Please do not revert to making diagnoses based on your beliefs. Please consult a professional practitioner and even seek a second medical opinion regardless whether you believe the depression to be endogenous or that the biology is the effect of a mindset.)
   Be ready to supply the appropriate encouragement to get started and keep going until they experience a difference. This support could even include help with the content of a programme, because if the depression is severe, people do not have the "motivation" to even want to think about what to do.

6. **Cognitive reframing: justification or comparison with an "even worse" scenario**. This strategy is useful for people skilled in how they say things, or when one has high credibility in the eyes of the person you are assisting,

like if you are a medical doctor or a psychiatrist. Othewise establish and maintain good rapport and be diligent in applying your listening skills. The recommended steps are:

a) Encourage the person to restrict the definition and judgement to a particular, circumscribed context. The implied message is that this judgement is relevant only to the agreed context and is not applicable to other contexts even if, on the face of it, they may appear to be similar. The discussion here involves getting the person's agreement on this contextual definition of which the emotion is a reflection.

   This is a key step, because if the person cannot accept this contextual definition with comfort, the rest of this strategy will not make an emotion-changing impact.

b) Together with the person, do a comparison with a similar, but worst-case version of this experience. The outcome of this step is to give the person another way of judging their experience. This review of their experience becomes a window of opportunity to come to another judgement, and resulting outcome, for which they can take responsibility.

c) If the redefining of the experience does not yield results, invite the person to do a constructive dissociation. This step requires the person to create a safe psychological distance between them and the details of the painful assessment.

   (This technique works best for people who favour making pictures as a way of thinking. People who mostly think in sounds or feelings will experience difficulty with this technique.)

ACTIVITY:

First, ask the person to imagine a picture of themselves at a distance, or as if they were on television. This step teaches the person to do what the brain does naturally when it reviews personal behaviour for the purpose of self-criticism or self-improvement. Encourage them to see some detail of their clothing or body language to help them to do this exercise comfortably. Paying attention to yourself from a distance activates a different thinking style and is a very powerful way of reducing the intensity of an emotion about the event.

Secondly, encourage them to now think about the event in exactly the same way as they have just been thinking about themselves. As they maintain this psychological distance, encourage them to explore what they can learn about the event, and about themselves, that they have not realised before. With your language, encourage them to approach the exercise with an attitude of inquisitiveness so that they can make an interesting discovery about themselves as an outcome. Inquisitiveness as a thinking style functions on the basis of psychological distance, and as long as they can maintain this attitude, they will not get caught up in the experience with its resultant immediacy of hurt.

Thirdly, take them through the procedure of a well formed outcome so that they can employ the discovery about themselves in a positive and constructive way.

    d)   If the redefining of the experience meets with the person's wholehearted approval, in other words, if the new definition is ecologically sound for the person, then you move on to a well-formed condition of an outcome, and a self-contract that the person is prepared and capable of taking responsibility for.

Change the thinking pattern or the judgement

Another way of helping with the change of an emotion is to deal with the message itself. (See more details in chapter 5.)

In a nutshell, the steps are:

- Agree on the relevant context for which the person needs emotional first aid and give it a name.
- What is significant about this experience?
- Agree on what the message is.
- Get to an outcome statement, or the alternative experience the person would like to have (with due consideration for the well-formed conditions of an outcome). How could the person think differently about the event so that it will change the message? Check that the new way of thinking about the event is ecologically sound.

When you start to identify the context and message, remember that this would specifically be that area of the person's life about which they are making the comparison, and have come to the conclusion that there is a gap between what is happening and what is possible.

A proposed way of exploring the contexts and messages with the person can include: (Please remember your listening skills as per chapter 6. This judgement and resulting pain might not necessarily make sense to you, but remember to pay attention to their message and listen long enough to hear their judgement and criteria.)

ACTIVITY:

As you begin to gather information about yourself, consider asking questions that apply at these different levels. At which levels are you making the comparisons?

What are you comparing at that level? You might not compare at all levels, so write only those ones that are relevant to you for this exercise.

- Environment refers to external factors that are either opportunities or constraints: these involve questions such as "where?", "when?", and "with whom?"
- Behaviour is made up of specific actions or reactions within the environment: questions here involve "what?"
- Capabilities and skills are about the knowledge and skills, the "how-to's" that guide and give direction to behaviour: these are the "how?"-questions.
- Beliefs and values provide the reinforcement (motivation and permission) to support or suppress your capabilities: here we ask the "why?"-questions.
- Identity factors determine your sense of self: in other words, questions involving "who?"
- Purpose goes beyond self-awareness to relate to the bigger picture about your mission: the questions here are "what for?" and "for whom?"

Activity (for more detail please review the section in Chapter 4 on Logical Levels):

As you begin to gather information about yourself consider asking questions that apply at these different levels. At which levels are you making the comparisons? What are you comparing at that level? You might not compare at all levels, write only those one's that are applicable to you for this exercise.

Environment refers to the factors that are external opportunities or constraints: answers the questions 'where?', 'when?', and 'with whom?'

Behaviour is made up of specific actions or reactions within the environment: answers the question what?'

Capabilities and skills are about the knowledge and skills, the 'how-to's that guide and give direction to behaviour: answers the question 'how?'.

Beliefs and values provide the reinforcement (motivation and permission) to support or deny your capabilities: answers the question 'why?'

Identity factors determine your sense of self: answers the question 'who?'

Purpose goes beyond self-consciousness to relate to the bigger picture about your mission: answers the questions 'what for' or 'for whom?'

In conclusion: Sadness or its extreme form – depression – has a clear message pointing to a significant and highly important "missing piece". You become aware of this missing piece as you make one or more comparisons: yourself against yourself, your sense of identity, within yourself and in relation to others, etc. Not only do comparisons create the missing piece, but it also gives it a very personal and unique significance. The homework we need to do here is how to fill the gap, or maybe endeavour not to even run this thought-virus programme at all.

CHAPTER 8

ANGER

Crossing the Line

From the point of view of emotional wellbeing, the question is not whether you should experience anger, but rather the appropriateness of your anger. I have heard a person say, after a bad experience, that they vow to never ever become angry again. This is not an ecologically sound comment because the person had just undertaken to eliminate a very useful piece of information about how they perceive and judge the world, other people in their world and information about themselves. Allow me to repeat: the issue is the appropriateness of your anger, and to respect anger in yourself and others rather than suppressing it or pretending it does not exist.

President Benjamin Franklin is known for saying: "Anger is never without a reason, but seldom a good one". It is very easy to succumb to the common pitfalls of denying or suppressing your emotions when you have remorse and feel that you had over-reacted or that your reaction was "over-the-top", often resulting in the resolve to never "be like that again".

But what then is appropriate anger? This is the question we will address in this chapter, while we learn about anger and how to be resourceful with your own anger messages. People who have a problem with their anger often confess that anger is the emotion they find most difficult to control. These people usually offer two possible explanations: either the speed with which they get angry or the intensity of their anger (when they get angry, they get very angry) makes it hard for them to control their anger.

Anger, like any other emotion, has a function – it is a message for the person about a judgement they have made in a particular context. What gives it the appearance of being different from other emotions is that, when it is out of control, it can motivate someone to hurt or destroy other people. Because of its potentially destructive influence, most societies take a grim view of anger. This, however, does not mean that anger is inherently bad. Anger is not the only reason why people kill, but it is the most notorious emotional excuse. Because of this potential for damaging other people, as well as different people's own comfort zones with respect to experiencing appropriate anger, they teach children "things" about anger. These "things" range from it is not allowed (to have it, to show it, to express it), right through to the judgement that people who become angry are a certain, "not nice kind" of person. Another devastating "lesson" that people can learn in childhood is that you don't have the right to be angry. These lessons can have devastating effects on self-esteem if their anger is met with the question, "who do you think you are?" and the implied answer, "nobody of significance". Over time this diminishing of significance, and anger about it, can lead to beliefs about how bad the person really is, because "nice people don't _______."

Anger as a message
The minimum message anger gives is that it reflects the violation of an important criterion for the person experiencing it. In this regard anger is no different from any of the other negative emotions because it reflects a negative experience from the negative evaluation of an event. Anger, however, takes on a few qualities which gives it the "bad name" it got through human history. To verify the experiential validity of what I am going to say, you might compare this with your own experience of anger. Before you read any further, please think of a time when you were well and truly angry and, by paying attention to your own anger, you will notice the following:

- It fills the mind.

Anger as an emotion seems to have the ability to reach a level of intensity that becomes "pre-occupying" very quickly. (The only other two emotions that can occupy the mind with similar speed are sexual feelings and surprises of happiness.)

- The intensity of the anger increases proportional to the amount of time spent thinking about the reasons for being angry.

Interestingly, most people experience this escalation through the modality or medium of internal dialogue, especially when it is used to self-righteously justify their anger, usually directed at somebody else. This normally includes listing all the reasons why you should be angry with the other person, and in the process of reviewing all of these reasons, you give yourself "permission" to get even angrier. All of this contribute to the escalation in intensity. Then, a second step can come in, and this is what makes anger the concern of people in any society, namely:

- It short-circuits the process of assessing the consequences of going into action (doing) – in this sense "anything" becomes possible.

When anger reaches a certain level of intensity in some people, they fixate on "doing" fueled by their anger, without any proper consideration for the effect of their angry actions, meaning they are more likely to "step over the line". It is not unusual to hear people make comments like "but did he/she not think what might happen when he/she did while they were that angry"? No, they did not do the necessary thinking into the future, and it is this "not thinking into the future" under the "influence" of intense anger that is called a "cognitive incapacity".

Why anger?

I am not sure this question can be answered fully; however, here are some ideas from my own clinical experience of why people respond with anger when their criteria have been violated:

They see no other way of addressing or augmenting the event/ transgression: people, especially men, with low self-esteem may experience a violation of their criteria as a "hopeless event" and don't see how they can influence the outcome or change the experience. "Low self-esteem" often tends to correspond with a low sense of self-efficacy. People who run these processes in their heads tend to experience events as if they are victims. Albert Bandura, a Stanford psychologist who has done a lot of research on self-efficacy, sums it up well:" People's beliefs about their abilities have profound effect on those abilities. Ability is not a fixed property; there is a huge variability in how you perform. People who have a sense of self-efficacy bounce back from failures; they approach things in terms of how to handle them rather than worrying about what can go wrong."

Optimistic people see a failure as due to something that can be changed so that they can succeed next time around, while pessimists take the blame for their failure, ascribing it to some lasting characteristic that they are helpless to change. The differing attitudes have profound implications for how people respond to life. Optimists see the setback as something that can be remedied. Pessimists, by contrast, react to such setbacks by assuming that there is nothing that they can do to make things go better the next time, and so do nothing about the problem.

When people experience a violation of their criteria, and they think with a pessimistic frame of mind (i.e. with a low sense of self-efficacy), this experience of having their "back against the wall" frequently leads to anger in men, and to submissive or "victim" attitudes in women. (These different reactions are learned in particular societies and are not inherent in the anger response of men and women.) This simply means that these people define the event in such a way that they cannot think of a way to cause a change, and the resultant anger is therefore a double message. Their anger becomes loaded with lots of other issues and frustrations. Their anger can say any combination of the following: my criteria have been violated, and I have no hope of making a difference; I am feeling helpless; I cannot do anything; what's the use of trying to make a difference; even if I try or say something it will not matter or change anything; etc.

- They have a conviction that if you are angry, people will give in and do what you ask, otherwise they will not do it for you: This belief is often formed fairly early in life and then reinforced by everyday experiences that provide

them with the "evidence" that this is a practical way of doing things – if
not the best way.

- Because they have been hurt, it is justification to hurt them back.
- It is a learned response that gets triggered by any negative experience and
  functions in the same way a reflex would operate – instantaneous and
  without thinking or considering another possibility in dealing with the
  unwanted experience.

Direction of Anger

Anger has another attribute that is unique to this emotion in that anger can be
directed either at yourself or to other people. To contrast this with any other
emotion, think of a particular feeling and notice who the feeling is directed at? Some
feelings will be about yourself, while other feelings will be about other people, but
the feeling is, in a sense, defined by its direction. Try to imagine redirecting the
emotion. You will find it is impossible to do so without the emotion losing its
inherent message or significance.

When determining which direction anger should be aimed at, the question of "who is
guilty" comes into play. If the person's low self-esteem includes a self-evaluation or
belief that they are inherently "bad", "worthless" or "not good", etc., they will
direct their anger at themselves as an act of non-acceptance of themselves. Their
self-directed anger reflects the message that they are at fault, and therefore they
deserve "it"; their just desserts for being so stupid, worthless, bad, no-good, etc. If,
however, they determine that the other person is at fault, they will, with much self-
justification, direct their anger at the other person who dared to be so _________.

What to do with Anger

When you want to help someone deal with their anger, please remember the
listening skills we discussed in Chapter 6. Their judgement and resulting pain might
not make sense to you, but remember that it is not about your pain. Pay attention to
their message and listen long enough to hear their judgement and criteria.

1) Distraction – pay attention to something else.

The technique of distraction is not new and works very well with children who insist
on having something their parents refuse to give at that moment. The level of your
absorption in the distraction will determine the effectiveness of this strategy.
Therefore the content of that which you will be paying attention to must have
enough of an interest for you to serve as a useful distraction. Furthermore, it also
helps if it can keep you actively, behaviourally busy. The more "demanding" this
activity is on your attention, the more effective will it "grab" or "tie up" your
attention, away from what made you angry.

2) Move to an environment where no more anger impulses are present and create an opportunity to relax.

This could be very useful in a marriage relationship where a couple might get stuck in an argument that is going nowhere. To stop for a moment and not only change the environment, but maybe also the activity, is an opportunity during which both partners can take a breather, relax and remember something useful and positive. This is an accepted technique during negotiation, and could have similar benefits in the context of a marriage, where it is equally important to sometimes just "take time out", and review some positives before you make another attempt to resolve the issue.

3) Change the thinking pattern, i.e. the justification for being angry. (See Chapter 5) Agree on the relevant context for which the person needs emotional first aid and give it a name.

- What is significant about this experience of anger?
- Agree on what the message of the person's anger is.
- Get to an outcome statement, or the alternative experience the person would like to have (with due consideration for the conditions for a well-formed outcome). How could the person think about the event differently in order to change the message? Check that the new way of thinking about the event is ecological.

4) Deal with the internal dialogue.

There are two kinds of techniques for dealing with the internal dialogue that, through the content and tone of justification, was intensifying the person's anger, namely to stop the justification and change the internal quality of the voice you use to say the justifying thoughts with.

a.   **Stop saying the justifying things to yourself.**

The first option is simply to stop. Then pay attention to something else and continue your internal dialogue about the other content that you are busy with. Sometimes, however, you are so furious that you don't want to stop your thoughts (some will people will call this "not being able to"), especially because you have all of these gazillions of "legitimate" reasons for really having the right to be angry. If it had not been for all these reasons, you would have stopped straight away, but you can't just stop. After all, this is something really important... You get the idea? This is exactly the time to stop thinking about the event.

Here are some additional ways to help you accomplish this task at those moments when it is difficult to stop justifying your anger:

- Once you make the decision to stop, apply the distraction rule without delay! As you make the first decision, immediately decide what you will be paying attention to in its stead. Remember, the mind cannot deal with "not doing", so help yourself by giving yourself an alternative train of thought.
- Change one or more components of your physiology as a way to emphasise to your brain that this mind–shift is to be taken seriously. One option is to turn your body slightly and think in another direction, as if you were listening for or looking at the new idea in a different place or physical location. Another way is to change your breathing pattern the minute you pay attention the content of the new idea.
- Typically, when you're angry, your breath is shallow and you only breathe in the upper part of your chest. Deliberately make your breathing pattern slower and breathe from the lower part of your chest to accompany the change in the content of your thoughts.
- Yet another way is to relax your shoulders and hands deliberately as you change your breathing and the content of your thoughts.

b. **Change the quality of your internal voice.**

Have you noticed how, when you talk to yourself, that your voice has the same qualities as when you speak aloud to someone? For example, when you are angry, your internal voice will have certain characteristics that go with being angry; you may talk fast, internally loud and your voice may come from particular place in your throat, etc.

Compare the tone of your voice when you are talking to yourself as if you were explaining something to a person you know, or when you think of sharing some good news with someone who is important to you.

Each of the examples will have its own tone or "voice signature", which is one of the ways in which you recognise what you are busy with on the inside, namely being excited, angry, loving, curious, etc. You can, therefore, change the tone by speaking slower, softer, or from a different part of your throat; and if you then also change the content of the thought, you can help yourself to make the switch.

Imagine that you are expressing your thoughts to somebody that you admire (and you are not angry with) and you are using them as a sounding board, and notice what "voice signature" would be applicable to him or her. Now use that tone to think your angry thoughts if you must, or change the content as you use this alternate tone of voice.

5) Talking it out or venting your anger.

The professionals call it catharsis or abreaction. Research "time after time, found that giving vent to anger did little or nothing to dispel it (though, because of the seductive nature of anger it may feel satisfying)." (Mallick and McCandless: "A Study of Catharsis Aggression." Journal of Personality and Social Psychology 4. 1966).

There may, nevertheless, be some specific conditions under which lashing out in anger does work: when it is expressed directly at the person who is the target, when it restores a sense of control or rights an injustice, or when it inflicts "appropriate harm" on the other person and gets them to change some grievous activity without retaliating. However, because of the incendiary nature of anger, this may be easier said than done.

6) Do the intervention to control anger as soon as possible.

The golden rule for any emotional self-control is to do it as soon as possible – especially with the emotions with which you are having a difficulty, either because they are too intense or are not appropriate for the events in which they occur. Please note that I am referring here to the emotions that occur as a pattern, or regularly; and it is with regards to the pattern that you want to make an adjustment. This is not to be seen as a technique for "getting rid" of an emotion, but rather to explore more ecologically sound emotional responses.

Help yourself

By the time you experience an emotional "pattern", your mind has already developed its own way of recognising the cues to which it responds with the practised emotion. To apply emotional control, the intention is to work with the same cues that trigger the emotion, to help you to control your emotional response to it. You will be surprised at how easy this is.

> **ACTIVITY:**
>
> Think of a situation in which you habitually become angry. Identify the cues in the event that, when you notice them, your mind immediately gives you the emotion that you want to control. These cues could be something you see, like the other person's face, or a certain expression on their face. It could be something you hear, like the other persons' voice, or even a particular quality to their voice.
>
> Once you have identified the cue, you can test it in the following way: if you think about it, you will either feel the emotion starting to occur, or you might even have the full emotion as if the person is present. This will be your confirmation that you have correctly identified the relevant cue.

By using the exercise for getting to a well-formed condition of an outcome (Chapters 3 and 5), be clear in your mind about which appropriate alternative response you want to have in that situation.

Once you have a response that is appropriate to the event and you have done your rehearsal so that you are comfortable to "switch it on" or "run" the new emotion, you are ready for this step. Think very briefly of the cue that you have identified in the previous step and then immediately and very rapidly shift your thoughts to the emotion you want to experience in stead of the original one...and spend a few seconds experiencing the chosen response. Clear your thinking by paying attention to something in your environment, and repeat the thought-shifting exercise, which is really what this step is: to very rapidly shift your thought from the cue to the new response as a way of teaching your brain what response is the favoured one.

Repeat this exercise until you feel the process comes naturally or "runs by itself".

If the cue triggers an intense, original response before you can call up the preferred response, then, in your thinking, you don't have to call the cue into your mind at all. It will work equally well if you anticipate the cue and do the "switch" even before you imagine the cue occurring in your mind.

The process would then go like this: imagine a point minutes or seconds before you would think of the cue, and immediately "switch", so that as the cue comes into your mind you already have the new "programme" in place to think with.

In conclusion: Anger has a legitimate place in your experience. Be respectful of yourself and pay attention to your anger, as it is a message about criteria that are being violated. The question is not whether you should have an angry response, but rather how your anger can be useful and ecological to both the people who are the subject of your anger, and to yourself and the values that you hold dear.

CHAPTER 9

TRAUMA

Mastering Severe Emotions

Trauma can result both from a single event, or a pattern of events, that is emotionally experienced as extremely intense and negative.

In everyday experience, however, we associate trauma with major, catastrophic events in people's lives, like serious motorcar accidents, rape, armed robbery, hostage situations, etc. In clinical experience, however, one also hears of instances where, for example, the cumulative effect of many little things or a series of events over a prolonged period of time had resulted in the same emotional intensity and pain as in the severe examples mentioned first.

Let me explain. People have reported that after many years in a particular situation, like a marriage or a parental home, in which they were repeatedly told negative things about themselves, they came to a point at which they made the profound decision that what they were told about themselves, namely, that they are unworthy or not nice people, is actually true. What a devastating conclusion to come to! The pain of being confronted with this "truth" is the same as "breaking your heart", or the horrible experience of the core of your being raped or destroyed. The effects of these kinds of experiences have all the mental attributes of trauma.

So what turns an experience into trauma? After decades of counselling people with all kinds of hurt, I am convinced that an experience becomes a trauma when the following six things happen in a person's mind. (We may even call it the preconditions of trauma.):

A drastic violation of an important, high-order criterion
Examples of high-order criteria, which, if they are violated in one incident or over a period of time (as a pattern), leaves a person with a sense of being traumatised, are: one's personal ("good") identity, one's personal significance, one's personal security (emotional and physical), one's personal self-worth, etc.

Whatever the nature of the incident to which a person is exposed, it takes on the quality of a trauma if any of their higher order criteria have been violated. This brings us to a vital point that is often overlooked in the research on trauma: not all experiences of violations of higher order criteria automatically produce trauma. The person had to have made a distinction about whether the criterion that was violated was of core importance or not; in other words, that their highest criterion was violated. Why is this distinction so important, you might ask?

Researchers love to predict which one of the core criteria of a person will produce trauma if violated. In my experience the reason why people experience events as traumatic or not are not always transparent or predictable.

There are many exceptions to the "rule". I am sure you can think of several examples of people who have had experiences that would have been "traumatic" for you, and yet they dealt with the event, irrespective of its intensity, in a way that could not be considered "traumatic" by any definition. (There are, of course, some who would cast doubt and insist that they are just suppressing their emotions, irrespective of what the person involved would say or do.) The fact that they are not traumatised is not necessarily a statement about their emotional competence (or lack thereof), but because they define the situation differently from you, and are therefore not traumatised by it.

This following example helps to illustrate this: Imagine that you were a member of a police service and that for one, even two years you had to serve in a riot-torn area. Your eight-hour shift is an exercise in survival during which you cannot afford to relax for one moment. When people approach you on the street, you don't know if they're innocent and genuinely just want to talk or ask advice, or pose a potential threat.

To stretch your emotional self-mastery further, your professional code as a police officer requires you to be polite and civil, if not friendly, which means that you also have to act as if you are not tense or suspicious. You have to contain your preparedness and impulse to protect yourself, with the full knowledge that you compromise "your edge" in the process of fulfilling the community service aspect of your duty.

Internationally, the number of police officers suffering from severe stress, given their stressful circumstances, is surprisingly low. Why? One of the reasons is that their definition of their work is different from what you and I imagine it to be.

When, over time, they do become stressed, those people report a corresponding change in their thinking about their police work. This change in definition means that important criteria are then being violated in the light of this new definition, and their intense emotional reaction, which only sometimes is traumatic in nature, reflects this new definition of theirs. (You can explore this point further by reading "Listening to the Emotional Message" in Chapter 6.)

Typical everyday emotional responses to the experience of having your criteria violated are anger, tension, crying, withdrawal, etc. After a few repetitions, your own rapid response to this kind of experience becomes learned behaviour which, over time, turns into your predictable preference. Thus, when one of your higher-order criteria becomes violated, you will have an intense emotional reaction to the event, but your response to the event and to your own emotion, would be acceptable to you – whether it is anger, withdrawal, or any of your rapid-response preferences.

However, when an experience becomes traumatic, these rapid-response strategies are not "switched on", or the decision is that they are not appropriate or preferred in this situation. You are then "left" with the intense experience and no mental "place to go". This is when you cross the threshold.

The pain crosses the "threshold of tolerance"
For you to experience an event as traumatic, not only does one or more of your core criteria have to be violated, but you also have to experience the event as exceedingly painful; so painful, in fact, that you feel that "it is more than I can take/handle".

This decision that it is "more than I can take/handle" reflects your judgement that the experience is so painful that it exceeds your available strategies for dealing with extremely painful of uncomfortable experiences. In clinical terms it is referred to as going through a threshold of tolerance, or going through an emotional threshold. My experience with helping people with severe emotional pain is that unless they come to this conclusion, they will not be "traumatised".

This emotional threshold is unique to each individual. I am not aware of any research that indicates that this threshold is an "objective", scientifically-proven point, but is rather based on an individual's internal assessment of how much can be tolerated. To emphasise: two decisions have to be taken for the experience of going through the emotional threshold to be a reality, namely, that existing strategies for dealing with a violation of one's criteria are not "switched on", and, the intensity of the experience is "more" than the person can handle.

People have internal mechanisms for recognising the kind and intensity of emotions they experience (see the previous chapter on recognising the coding of your emotions), and it is by using these internal recognition cues that a person will recognise both the meaning or message of an emotion, and also make the decision whether the intensity is too much or not.

Over generalising the message of the experience (as the definition or meaning of the event) is taken out of the context in which it happened and generalised to other contexts.

This means that the definition or meaning given to situation A is generalised and also applied to situations B and C, which might have some resemblance to A, and because of this resemblance and subsequent generalisation, is experienced as the same. In time, this generalisation is extended further and further as more events are incorporated, even those that have only a single minor component in common become included, and therefore, elicits the same intense emotional response. It might go so far that the person decides "all of life" or "all people" are like that. Because the response is so basic, the brain seems to apply a different set of rules as it generalises. Needless to say that the generalisation leads to over-sensitivity and over-reaction.

This generalised definition is eventually turned into a belief system through the mechanism of language. (See point 6 below for more on how this generalisation leads to a belief about the cause and effect of the negative event.) Once a person has a belief about how this experience is a "way of life", they use it to justify to themselves and others that the way they defend and protect themselves is not only necessary, but appropriate.

The internal strategy for the negative experience becomes shortened and more "automatic"

Because the brain has such an incredibly fast learning mechanism, once you have run a thought pattern a few times, it runs faster and faster, to the point where it becomes automatic. One of the best examples where you can see this characteristic of the brain's ability to learn on display, is when you look at how much faster someone who is an expert at a particular skill can perform certain tasks compared to a beginner.

The increase of speed is not only because the mind "gets used to" the pattern and therefore easily runs a familiar pattern, but also starts to create "short-cuts" in running the now-familiar pattern. In the case of trauma, a person eventually needs very little stimulation to completely and very rapidly recall the intense, negative experience.

Something as little as a smell, sound, seeing something, or a feeling which in some way resembles the negative one, could be sufficient for the mind to conclude that this is like the original experience, and then the person is instantaneously "flashed back" into that experience.

Because of the way that the brain uses generalisation for rapid learning, this function can also lead to a kind of "over-enthusiastic" response through faulty generalisation by equating even the slightest similarities of subsequent situations to the original event even though they are, in fact, not like the original event at all. Often times the brain uses such minimal cues for its rapid-response facility to a perceived threat that they fall outside of conscious awareness, and the person is then on the receiving end of "uncalled-for flashbacks" that "just seem to happen".

Instantaneous mid-brain (the "home" in the brain for emotional responses) **response** is faster than any cortical/thinking strategy. Furthermore, the intensity of the emotional evaluation reduces your ability to make finer distinctions and comparisons, and while this is happening, you are only thinking about survival, coping, and maintaining some resemblance of your highest criteria.

This reduced ability to make the finer, maybe more appropriate distinctions and comparisons for proper evaluation and response is an additional contributing factor to the generalisations and enhances the very vivid recall of the events.

Time shift
When you think about the experience (e.g. when you have a flashback) you remember it as if you are in the event in the here and now, as if it is happening at this very instant.
This is an example of the negative side of one of the brain's marvellous capacities when it comes to the experience of time, specifically, how not to be in the moment, or the here and now. When you recall an event as if it is happening to you right now, two important experiential attributes are relevant, namely, the "time shift" that is taking place, and the total reality of the event that repeats itself.

This time shift that takes place is often so complete that you "forget" that you are remembering from the here and now. As far as you are concerned, you are there and then in the experience, with no awareness of the present moment. Should you have mastered the event, you would be able to distinguish and be aware that you are remembering from the here and now. The ability to remember that you are "just" remembering is a very important experiential component for mastery. It brings with it the awareness that the event rightfully belongs to the past, that it is really over and that you have, in fact, survived it. These realisations – that it is really over and that they've survived the incident – often lead important experiential breakthroughs in the treatment of trauma.

It is important to understand what is happening here. When someone thinks about an experience in a manner as if it is happening to them right now, the experience is still "ongoing", and the respite after the reliving of the experience does not include the "reality" that it is from their past. Even if they mouth the words that they know it is in their past, the experiential reality of what happens during the flashback or recall is "more real" than them saying that it is over. Therefore, the revision of their own experience is lagging behind what they know "intellectually".

This leads us to two very important points in terms of the total reality of the event that repeats itself: the person remembers the event, as well as their personal capabilities, in terms of how they were at that time. Therefore, remembering from that position of more limited capability is a contraindication for the claim that you have to re-experience intense negative emotional events in order to heal.

The recalling of the reality of the event means remembering the event from the viewpoint of how the person was at that time, including experiential factors like their age and corresponding capabilities, feelings of disempowerment that they experienced in the situation, etc. So, in the reliving the event, all the experiential components that contributed to make the event the trauma it was, repeats itself, with the same overwhelming sense of "this is too much". This means, for example, that people remember the event with all the "as if's" that was relevant at the time, like "as if" they are the same age as when the event happened; "as if" they have the same inability to influence the situation now, as they did then.

Reliving the original event with the hope of resolving it is therefore, actually just a sure way of hurting the person repeatedly with questionable effect upon their ability to master the emotional experience. One wonders at the extensive period required for some of the treatment methods, as well as the subjects' often extreme discomfort during the therapy process, and whether this is not an indication that the mind is rebelling against it being battered further in the name of healing.

Extensive research in the field of academic performance indicates that people learn optimally when their minds are at ease, they have a sense of mastery and are comfortable with the process to be employed during the exam (read "event"), etc. Yet, there is a dogged belief that when we talk about emotional learning and dealing with pain, the conditions for and the brain's ability to learn, to process, to gain new perspectives and to update, are suddenly different. Therefore, the erroneous conclusion then goes, repeat the hurt with all the restrictions that research indicates is not good for learning, and expect that learning will occur – ergo, two wrongs make a right.

Negative experience can become the source of a belief about self, others and the world.

Beliefs have the function in the mind of capturing explanations about "how the world works". Beliefs can be put into three categories, namely beliefs about oneself in relation to oneself, beliefs about oneself in relation to other people, and beliefs about oneself in relation to the world. This "in relation to..." includes an explanation of how one imagines or "knows" the phenomena to work, with or without the impact it has on oneself.

Understanding is frequently associated with being able to verbalise the insight, or understanding a phenomenon through the medium of language. The person endeavours to understand the experience through asking questions like "why", and/or "what caused it", expecting to come up with a "logical" answer. "Logical" is sometimes just the name for being able to "say" or articulate a belief or opinion.

The nature of the questions asked would lead the person to formulate an answer that they believe to be "true" in explaining the experience to themselves. Typically, this answer to the question of "why" will be in the form of "________ causes ________". This belief can become ingrained the more the person thinks about it and comes up with the same answers.

Beliefs also become entrenched the more they are challenged, because as people find more reasons to defend their beliefs, they give themselves more reasons to believe in them, to the point where they are not prepared to consider any opinion that is not a confirmation of the belief they (now) have about the experience.

When the person's thinking has "solidified" into a belief system about self, others and the world, the belief system becomes characterised by:

It being interpretive rather than descriptive
The belief, rather than being an explanation or description of the event only, now includes a judgement about the goodness or (mostly) badness of not only the event, but everything that is inferred from it. This leads to conclusions like the world is a bad or dangerous place, all people are out to hurt you, it is never safe to trust anybody, etc.

Their understanding of the reason for the event is seldom positive and contributes to their sense of being unsafe. Their signification of the world as unsafe, its people of uncertain character, combined with their own sense of disempowerment or lack of self-efficacy, feeds into the generalisations and increases the potential for a very unhappy and restrictive life.

Until they update their experience – and, especially, restore their sense of self-efficacy – they consider this as the way to experience life, people, self and the world (depending on the extent of the generalisations and the effective range of their belief system). The experience they have had provides them with compelling "evidence" that this is the nature of life. No arguments or information to the contrary, irrespective of the expert source, is sufficient to convince the person who has experienced trauma that the world is different from their "knowledge" about it.

Negative and/or disempowering statements about their identity and competence
Inevitably, an experience that leaves a traumatic "residue", will be characterised by acute feelings of disempowerment. One of the intense negatives that contribute to an experience being coded as traumatic is the fact that, at the time of the experience, the person was a "victim". The experience of a victim is one of very low self-efficacy, a strong sense of disempowerment or helplessness, and being a passive recipient of whatever this negative event entails. The destructive correlate of this component of the experience is that people then define themselves in terms of this experience. Some examples of this definition of self that result from these intense, negative emotional experiences are:

- I am the kind of person who deserves that.
- It is punishment for the way I am as a person (e.g. selfish, uncaring, not loving enough, not doing enough of the right things for other people, etc.).
- I am not worth to be treated in another way.
- I am incompetent.
- I am not capable of dealing with things like that.

The common denominator in all of these statements is they reflect an erroneous definition of self because they take their experience of and response to a particular event as a total definition of self, and also add a negative interpretive value to it. The trap that people fall into with these types of "I am" statements is that they are experienced as so final that the possibility of adding to one's competence has decidedly been cancelled out. "This is the way I am" is implied with a corresponding sense of helplessness at the perceived finality of the negative state. "Nothing can be done about me or these kinds of events", is the erroneous conclusion; as if people cannot change or learn to be more competent or effective.

Its projected relevance into the far future
They expect that the rest of their lives merely offers variations to the theme of this intense, negative emotional experience. What was defined for the person during the traumatic event in a sense becomes the standard for similar events "forever more".

The person now also generalises through time, into the future, as opposed to seeing the event in the context of the time it occurred.

In conclusion: What turns an intensely negative emotional experience into a trauma is what the person does on the inside with an event that violated their core or highest criteria.

By employing the mental strategies described above, the person becomes a co-creator of their trauma. It is not only the event itself that creates the trauma. It is mostly what the event means to the person, which is a deciding factor in whether they will code or process the experience as a trauma or not.

As we have established in previous chapters, emotions are messages about a person's ongoing decisions (to be more specific, their distinctions and comparisons), made at an incredibly rapid pace. These distinctions and comparisons are in relation to the self, other people and the world. The intensity of an emotion reflects the importance the person ascribes to the experience, and the type of emotion (i.e. positive or negative) reflects the value component of the judgement, namely the goodness or badness of the experience as compared with one's internal criteria.

Having made the decision that the event's seriousness and intensity exceed available strategies for dealing with the violation of their criteria, the person then could "create" the trauma by:

    a.   Experiencing the intensity as pushing past their threshold;

    b.   Generalising the experience to other life events;

    c.   Creating rapid, automatic responses to the generalisations through thought repetition (not unlike mental rehearsal);

    d.   Being totally immersed in and reliving the experience as a current reality, forgetting that, at that moment of recall, their experience is one of reflection, a process of remembering an event from the past, not an event that is presently unfolding;

    e.   Generating a belief system about self, others and the world in an endeavour to explain the event and exclusively using the trauma as the data source for these beliefs.

You may have found this chapter to be more in the "telling" than the experiencing format, and that is quite true. One reason for that is that a precondition I insist on being met in working with trauma, is ensuring the emotional safety of the person. If you have been traumatised, you might find useful techniques in this book, but, please heed my call to rather ask a qualified NLP practitioner to guide you through the process.

CHAPTER 10

WORRY

— What is Going to Go Wrong Next?

Have you noticed that when you experience a particular emotion, you also pay attention to a certain period of time that seems to "belong" to the emotion? Let me share some examples with you:
When you think of feeling guilty, your attention goes to an event from the past.
When you think of feeling anxious, your thoughts go to the future, to an anticipated event that is yet to happen (even though it might be a repeat of a previous event that you are concerned about).

When you think of a person whom you love and think about a particular aspect of your love for them, you may find your thoughts going to a specific time or event, which could be past, present or future.

If you recall any emotion you have had as if it is happening to you right now, you may, as you become fully aware of the emotion, notice that your thoughts will go in a certain direction through time, which is determined by when the incident happens with regards to the emotion.

While this time-directed aspect of emotion might seem obvious, surprisingly few people realise the importance of this factor. It plays a crucial part in knowing what outcomes to set for yourself if you want to change the content or message of an emotion. It is important to remain aware, for instance, that worry is directed at an anticipated event in the future.

A Way of Thinking

People who are good at worrying are frequently not appreciated by those around them, especially if those around them have reasons for being excited or enthusiastic about something. The good worrier comes across as being unmotivated or killjoys, out to "spoil the fun with their negative attitudes" about what can go wrong. They have earned themselves the reputation of "if you want to be convinced something will not work, then tell it to X and they will confirm your doubts a hundredfold".

Good worriers are a rare breed who are usually under-appreciated for the contributions that they can potentially make. How can we understand and appreciate them? What worriers are good at, is paying attention to how things can go wrong.

From any piece of experience or learning given to them, the first unconscious question that wings through their mind is "what can go wrong?" As a result of processing information in this particular way, they ask questions about the event or make the kind of comments that "earn" them the reputation for being negative. The comments often come in the form of:

"Yes, but ________."
"We have tried this before and it didn't work."
"What if something goes wrong?"
"It will not work, and I can't tell you why; it is just a gut feeling."

Their intention is not to be negative, but to honestly bring up the concern in their minds. In a real sense they are asking for the reassurance that the necessary contingencies will be thought of in time before it goes wrong or one has wasted effort. A history of being rejected for their worry, for expressing their thoughts, contributes to how they sometimes present this information in a way that is not appropriately tactful or acceptable to their audience.

We are dealing here with an attention strategy which functions as a habitual way of thinking, which some psychologists call an "away from" thinking preference. It simply means that these people want to avoid the problems that they foresee and are, in effect, asking for reassurance. It is often said that people who worry a lot, spend a lot of time being apprehensive about what might go wrong, even though it might not, or it seldom does. One could, very plausibly, conclude that worriers live in a future which might, or might not, come true. You could say they are permanent residents of the land of "in case". From their perspective, they have a legitimate concern that things will go wrong. If it didn't, or if they could be sure that it wouldn't, they would be as carefree as everybody else. But, they know different... In fact, they have a conviction that something is going to go wrong, which is why they worry.

The effect of worrying is, however, not necessarily positive. If worrying leads to the next step, namely constructive problem solving, then this would be an unqualified good strategy to apply during certain circumstances, but worry can, and does, easily go wrong. Here are some cognitive errors that worriers often make:

Uncalled for worrying
When asking what can go wrong becomes the question of choice, this preferred thinking pattern starts running automatically. They often foresee problems because of their automatic way of thinking, usually before they have considered the situation carefully (if at all). This thought pattern would be the same as when a person sees a snake in the grass which, upon closer inspection, turns out to just be a piece of rope.

Or, if you're alone at home at night and are startled by a sound in the dark house and immediately think of danger. Depending on the intensity of this initial fear response, you might act on the "truth" of it without first establishing the facts. If the fear response is manageable, you might take a deep breath and try to verify whether the sound signals danger or was maybe just caused by the cat bumping something off the coffee table. The worry-equivalent of this mistaken definition follows the same pattern: the situation is defined as something that can go wrong, and the immediate response is to start mentally rehearsing all the possibilities of how wrong it can go ... and the worrier is off and away in worry mode.

Worrying about "everything"
This happens when people tend to generalise the "what" and/or the "when". The minute they identify some similarity with an event they have experienced before, this new event is automatically seen as "like" the reference experience, and is therefore charged with things that can go wrong. Having made this first, automatic generalisation about how this event is "like" the reference experience, they then stop making comparisons or do any further thinking about differences, and immediately go into thinking "away from". An increasing amount of cues gets the person to run their worry strategy. (As an interesting aside, this is an everyday occurring thought pattern that helps us to take shortcuts in our decision making based on how we anticipate or predict things or events to be similar. It is also the basis for racial, religious and sexual prejudice – making snap decisions about who people are because of certain features like skin colour, religious attire or sexual attributes, without verifying that the individual "fits" the category.)

Missing out on the good news
It is common knowledge that people pay selective attention to the contents of internal and external events. Imagine your mind is like a television screen, and the span of your attention is what you can hold on your screen. Selective attention is what you have unconsciously chosen to pay attention to. All the content of a particular event is stored and linked to the event, but you would pay attention to only parts of it at any one time.
What you pay attention to – which we so glibly refer to as "my choice" – is determined by an incredible range of variables, ranging from your mood at the moment, to your purpose in thinking about the event, to what is important (i.e. your values), to you how you are now in reference to the event, etc.

Unfortunately this very useful function can also lead to problems when what is omitted could lead to a redefinition of the meaning of the event.

People have preferred ways of thinking in certain events – what you choose or prefer to pay attention to, namely, the pictures, or sounds, or feelings in reference to a particular event. In some events you might have a preference to think in pictures, in others to pay attention to the sounds or what someone was saying, and sometimes you direct your attention to how you were feeling during the event. This preference continuously shifts, not only because of context, but also because you may have reason to start paying attention to the event in different ways or thinking modalities.

The rule is: the more modalities (i.e. pictures, sounds, feelings, smell and taste) I pay attention to, the more information I have about the event, which leads to more options when thinking about the event.

Say, for example, that you have just been introduced to a stranger, you would typically pay attention to them in your preferred modality, for instance, what they look like, or maybe what their voice sounds like, or what you are feeling at that moment. (People very seldom pay attention to more than modality at a time and tend to stay with their preferred modality of the moment, unless they have reason to pay attention in another modality).

You can now form an impression of the person based on your "one modality" impression, or you can expand your range of options for getting to know the person by systematically and sequentially paying attention to the other kinds of information about the person by merely shifting your attention to the other modalities. Let's say you start with a visual of the person and, what you see at first, is a fairly unfriendly person. You may then shift your attention to listening to their voice, and you hear a different quality of the person in their voice.

By now, you might start thinking that instead of being unfriendly, this might just be a serious person. After a while, you notice your feelings and might be pleasantly surprised that you quite like the person. (Then, of course, you will find people who insist that their first modality perception is accurate and complete, with no need to update their judgement! They will quite probably be asking you real soon to help with the disappointment of having interpreted somebody the wrong way).

Please note, it is only in exceptional, and in all likelihood intimate, circumstances when you will update your information by what a person smells and tastes like. These two modalities are very useful for building up an appetite, but are not standard tools for people to get to know each other with.

The Good and the Bad News about Worrying

I have yet to come across somebody who enjoys worrying, even though someone who worries a good deal spends a lot of time at it.

Why do they do it? For them, it is a necessary thing to do, given their conviction that something is going to go wrong in the future. It is in this mental rehearsal of potential problems, projected into the future, where one will find the partial payoff that reinforces the habit of worrying.

Specifically, worries are ways to deal with potential threats, through rehearsal of the potential unfavourable outcomes.

The good news

Our ability to project ourselves into a future that has not happened yet is such an integral part of the human make-up that we take this remarkable ability for granted. In the field of business, this is the domain of strategic thinking, wherein strategists try to understand the future in such a way that the appropriate contingency planning can be made in time for potential events that might impact on their business.

Futurists, of which Alvin Toffler is probably the best-known writer in the field, describe where societal and cultural habits and value-trends are leading to in the future: how it will affect and change our lives.

Life insurance companies cater to your wish to plan for the future when they encourage you to plan appropriately for your finances "in the event that should happen."

Married couples who don't like each other anymore, can't wait for the time when the kids are out of the house so that they can do whatever they think is going to be better than being married to each other.

Managers are complimented and sought after for their ability to "foresee" a problem and take precautionary action to prevent accidents, or avoid costly mistakes.

Lovers can't wait for the time when "we are always together", because they already anticipate some of the things they will be sharing with such a compelling reality that their hormones go a bit funny as they think about it.

The key difference in peak performers in any domain of life, and the rest of the people, are that the dreams of peak performers are not wishes, but have a passion and a compelling reality to it that makes it a driving force in their lives. They can already see it, hear and feel the achievement of it as if it is happening to them now, even if, in reality, it could be a significant time into the future!

This ability to anticipate future concerns forms the basis of the positive dynamic for the person who worries. Projecting themselves into the future place where the things are going wrong can allow the person (like the strategist, or the excellent manager mentioned above), to plan ahead and be ready with a solution to the anticipated contingency. Or, to do what it takes to minimise, if not to stop, the envisioned effects of the event. However, more often than not, this is also where the negative dynamic comes into play.

The bad news

People can get so involved in worrying that they only worry. Worrying is what they do. They can worry in spirals that repeatedly get them to reach the same point in their thinking. Worrying can also go awry through an overly-zealous mental preparation for an anticipated threat, like when worry thoughts lead to "what-if scenarios" if scenarios" of even bigger catastrophes. Worry becomes bad news when it does not lead to a solution or contingency planning, and the exercise of worrying leads to "nought but constant worrying". They may even get very upset because they are worrying in the first place, or because of the way they worry. The solution for these people cannot simply be "don't worry, be happy" as the popular late '80s pop song prescribed, but rather to combine worry with problem-solving and then, crucially, letting go.

Intensity

The intensity level of your worry is indicative of your assessment of the importance of, as well as your preparedness or competence for dealing with, the event. The more important it is to you, the higher the intensity of the worrying. In the same way, if it is important to you and your judgement is that you are not ready for it, or not competent to deal with it in a way that will meet with your criteria, the level of intensity of your worry will be higher than if it was less important.

You might want to test this in your own experience: think of time when you had one of those nagging worries that occasionally intruded onto your awareness. In retrospect, thinking about that example, you may notice that it was not an important worry (i.e. not something had significant implications for you or important people in your environment). If it had been an important worry, your mind will not let you off that easily. Your mind will signal the importance of the anticipated event or calamity both through intensity and repetition (repeatedly bringing the feeling, plus or minus the thoughts, into your awareness).

When the duration and/or the intensity exceed the person's threshold, the person is prone to "neural hijacking" and the attention fixates itself on very specific content. This is when the typical bad news components of worrying dominate the person's thinking.

One of the best examples of "neural hijacking" is spiral-type thinking: thinking the same worry thoughts again and again. No matter how hard they try to stop doing this, they keep coming back to the same thoughts being replayed on a never-ending loop in their minds.

In Emotional Intelligence, Goleman (p.66") refers to some examples where this pattern has taken on severe or clinical proportions: "for the phobic, anxieties rivet on the feared situation; for the obsessive, they fixate on preventing some feared calamity; in panic attacks, the worries can focus on a fear of dying or on the prospect of having the attack itself. In all these conditions, the common denominator is worry run amok."

It is not unusual for some people to worry about some of the effects or experiential components of their worrying. Someone might, for instance, worry that their constant worrying might cause them to have a heart attack. Alternatively, they mistake some of the somatic signals of worrying for warning signs of an imminent heart attack and then start worrying about dying. They may also worry that worrying will lead to exactly that which they want to avoid, whether it be a heart attack, an ulcer, uncomfortable heart palpitations, etc. Worry is an experiential cluster of thoughts and feelings, and the person can get stuck in worrying about any one of the components that make up the experience of worrying.

A word of caution: because the experiential components of worry overlap with indications of very serious heart or brain conditions, a sudden onset of excessive or constant worrying needs to be clinically examined and not merely seen as only an exercise of dealing with an anticipated unwelcome future.

Worry – the message
Waking up in the middle of the night is a more benign example of worry gone wrong. As we established above, if the worry is important enough the mind is not just going to let it go away; it will ask, even demand, attention (like in the examples of worry gone amok). Waking up with a worry is message that you have not given the appropriate thought to the message, that the message is still valid and is not going to go away until there is no reason for the message to be "displayed" anymore. In other words, your brain is not convinced that the work is done satisfactorily yet. Until the message of confidence or completion is experienced, the worry message will intrude on occasions, sometimes as a very unwelcome guest in terms of timing or intensity.

The message of worrying could be some of the following:
    a.   The person is anticipating that something will go wrong in the future;

b. this something concern values that are important enough for them to need to worry about it;

c. the message may refer to the person's judgement that they expect they will not satisfy their own criteria for that event;

d. the criterion they fear they will not meet is that they won't cope as they want or should.

In other words, worry indicates that the person has made an advance judgement that they will not be able to respond, or if they do, that this response might not be ecologically sound.

How to Deal with Worrying

Pattern interrupt, because "when worry is allowed to repeat over and over unchallenged, it gains in persuasive power" (Borkovec: p69 in Goleman, op cit.). The following steps are ways of "getting out of the feeling" so that you can consider alternatives. Some typical ways of doing this with worrying are:

Change what you are thinking about: if the worry is still in its incubational stages, like when it is just starting to happen and is at an intensity level which still gives you easy freedom to decide what you want to think about, change the content of your thinking. Typically, worry refers to an incomplete process; it indicates that a problem has been identified, but not solved yet. It is an early-warning system about an issue in the future that requires more thinking on your part. Therefore, having thanked the worrier part of you, be aware that you are in the process of finding a solution for what to do about the worry.

Change how you are thinking: Pay attention to the way in which you think your worry thoughts so that you can alter it. When you worry, you are usually already in the situation. One way of changing that is to "step out" and imagine you are thinking about the worry from a distance, as if it is somebody else's worry that you are assisting them with. For instance, if you mostly think in pictures when you worry, then it might help to imagine the worrying incident on a screen, as if watching a movie. If worrying is the result of what you say to yourself, change the internal tone so that you can get a sense that this conversation is about to be solved.

Change your posture: Each of us has a "worry posture". By changing the body language of worrying, you give yourself the opportunity to lessen the intensity of the worry so that you can work toward the solution. The change might be in your posture itself, or in the way you breathe, or going from pacing up and down to sit rather.

Ask "reality" questions; challenge the content of the thought: This step will enable you to get to a definition of the problem that you can work with, and to avoid getting into "shoulds" or "maybes" that are only issues because you are worried or afraid.

Some questions about the size or importance of the worry that can help you to define the worry:

- Is the worry really as big as I am thinking now? Can I reduce the size of the worry by thinking about the pieces that make it up? What are those pieces? Write them down, one piece or aspect per page (so that you leave room for ideas for possible actions and solutions).
- Are the consequences I am anticipating inevitable? Be specific about each of the consequences: what are they and how will it happen? Who will be involved? What will be involved? Write them down, one per page (so that you leave room for ideas for possible actions and solutions).
- Which aspects of the event have you maybe not considered yet and which, if you pay attention to it, allows you to think differently about the event?

Constructive worry: It is important to make two distinctions to help with the process of finding solutions: Firstly, what are the options for what can/has to happen in the world, and secondly, what are the options for what you can do on the inside?

"In-the-World" options: To consider the options for what has to happen concerning other people, things, information, activities, or places it is helpful to think whether these are things you can and have to do alone. Options might include doing it with somebody, going for advice first, asking a go-between, etc.

"Inside" options: This involves things that have to happen internally for you to prepare for and deal with the worry. Naturally, it includes thinking and feelings. Since your worry in this case has announced itself through the signalling of an emotion, you might want to focus on how to feel in preparation for, and during the occurrence of the worry. The method to get oneself aligned to do the inside thinking and feeling to help solving the worry, is to use the process for well-formed conditions of an outcome, discussed in a previous chapter.

> **ACTIVITY:**
>
> **Step 1:** How can I think or feel differently from what I am currently experiencing?
>
> **Step 2:** If I imagine that I am already experiencing that which I have thought of in step A, what do I feel, see and hear on the inside, which will be part and parcel of the difference?
>
> **Step 3:** When, where and with whom do I want to experience this?
>
> **Step 4:** How does having this experience fit with my highest values in this situation? How does it fit with my definition of myself? Will there be a price to

pay, for me? For other people? If yes, please review the contents of step 1, and see if you can make any changes that will take care of the concerns in step 4. If not, what other outcome would do the same job for you, but without the price? Now, go through steps 2 to 4 again, and again, until you are happy with the outcome.

When you are caught in the snare of worrying, it might not be easy to do these things, but maybe you just need a guide to walk you through the process so that you can do the steps unhindered. If all else fails, do not hesitate to go speak to another wise person, like your minister or a professional psychologist.

In conclusion: To worry is to have a concern for the future, specifically how something will go wrong. Here is the rub: "will" go wrong rather than "can" go wrong. There is typically such a strong conviction that goes with this thought that the emotional response is a genuine concern, a "will"-certainty rather than a "can"-possibility. Raising concerns about this element or issue in the future is used by wise people as the final stage in thinking or planning. The excellent research by Gabrielle Oettingen (reported in her book, Rethinking Positive Thinking) is good scientific proof that getting excited, or motivating yourself with the "secret" and positive thinking without considering potential obstacles, can set you up for possible failure and lack of resilience. Pay attention to the worry, and then complete the formula: what can/is to be done?

Worries, though uncomfortable, are for smart people, since it means you are thinking ahead. Now, complete the process by being prepared with a solution.

CHAPTER 11

FEELING GOOD

— Emotional Balance

The following exercise is useful to help you to identify the emotional choices you have made over a certain time period so that you can assess it and learn from this pattern in the hope that it can, ultimately, form part of an effort to make better choices, or to help you make it work better for you.

The exercise takes 20-30 minutes, but the insights you will glean from it are well worth the investment of time. So without further ado, simply answer the following questions:

1. Which emotions have you experienced during the past month? List the emotions in two columns: positive emotions in one, and negative emotions in another column. Try to make the list as complete as you can, even if an emotion was present only briefly or not very intensely. (If you have trouble remembering the emotions, think back on the events of the past month and recall which emotions you experienced before, during and after these events.)

2. How many positive, and how many negative emotions did you experience? What is your "feeling good"-ratio during this period?

3. Do you recognise a pattern when certain emotions occur? This question brings the "when" into focus to help you to develop awareness of which messages you experience in which situations and/ or contexts.
    Please note if there is a pattern when the emotions occur. Let's say, for example, that before you even have a meeting with person X, you already find yourself wondering what is going to go wrong. This anticipation of "wrong", even if it may be justified, might very well create a certain expectation and, along with it, form part of a self-fulfilling prophecy.
    Now, upon reflection, can you balance the emotions by thinking of another message and experience that might be more useful to you than this one?

4. If you had to select the "typical" emotions for this period of time, and imagined they were messages sent to you from yourself, what are you communicating to yourself? What is the message you are giving yourself? Please write down an answer for each of the emotions. Remember that the same emotion may have a different message in each situation.
    What would a more useful message be in each of the different situations, i.e. a message that is realistic, but allows you to have options to consider

and gives you permission to be the best version of yourself? Or, alternatively, if the current message(s) in certain situations are hindering rather than helping, what message(s) would then be more useful?

5. How generally can this message be applied? In other words, is the message only applicable to some, or many situations and people? Furthermore, are these messages really the only option? Consider doing a "reality" check and ask yourself what other message(s) might be more helpful across the range of situations – if you have to generalise?

6. What message(s) are you not giving yourself that you would want to do more often or more intensely? In which situations would you want to apply the message? What would the benefits or, conversely, price be to pay, if you had to change the message? If there is a price to pay: is there an appropriate alternative option that sees you avoiding paying a price in these situations? How else could this be approached?

7. Up to this part of the exercise we have used the time-frame of one month. For a deeper understanding and to see how representative it is of your general emotional experience, you might want to cast your gaze further, say for the past quarter, or the last year?

If you wish to work on the practical or functional side of these emotional patterns, you can also answer these questions:

8. Do these emotions serve you well? Do they help or hinder you in achieving outcomes you have committed yourself to? What would you like to see, both for you and the other people involved?

9. Is this range of emotions the best way for you to be, and do they express the best version of yourself? Does the range of emotions that you experience, and the messages that go with them, help or hinder you in expressing the best version of you? Can you utilise your best strategies/skills in the circumstances where you are experiencing a specific emotion in a particular situation?

Remember that emotions do not only influence our thinking in terms of "what" we think, but also "how" we think.

ACTIVITY:
Say, for example, you are driving on the highway and somebody cuts in front of you, causing you not only to hit the brakes, but also provokes your anger. How then, would you act in this situation? What would the thoughts be that accompany the anger? And here is the crucial question: are these thoughts helping or hindering to you in this situation?

If the same incident should happen five or 10 minutes from now, would those same thoughts help to prepare you to deal effectively and safely with the second or a possible third situation? If your emotions and thoughts were helpful in the first situation, then dealing with situation number two would be easier. You might decide to be more alert or keep a closer watch on the cars around you, watch your own following distance more closely, etc.

But if your thoughts and reactions were actually a hindrance, you might experience the second situation as more intense, which may further reduce your effectiveness. Rather than adapting your driving pattern to the circumstances, you might instead harden your attitude, trying

to minimise your following distance in an effort to prevent anyone from cutting in front of you, thereby actually putting yourself and others more at risk.

10. Will always being in a positive state be the best way for you to achieve the kind of life you would like to live? It your answer is a simple yes, then it is easy; then the "other side" of not feeling good must be the answer – that is the missing piece in your life. As you did with question 9 above, test how having positive emotions 24/7 would be and ask yourself, "how does it serve me?"

Do not be surprised if you discover that there are times when a positive emotion is not the best in a particular situation. In certain circumstances, a negative emotion allows you to behave more appropriately in that context than a positive emotion. For example, some people have difficulty speaking their minds or being assertive and, instead of respectfully verbalising their thoughts or offering a fairer solution, decide rather to keep quiet to keep the peace or to avoid "causing a problem". While pseudo peace will reign, for the moment, it may, however, create the false expectation that this illusion will be okay in the future as well. And of course it won't be, because it will "crop up" again and they would be expected to dance to the same tune, with the same outcome.

Frequently, these outcomes are not good or ecological for the player who initiates the "let's be happy, and dishonest" scenarios. Perhaps you can think of a time when, instead of permitting a negative emotion, you insisted on feeling good – and take note of what the ultimate outcome was.

An example might be a time where the more honest reaction would have been frustration, anger, disappointment, etc. as the more authentic message in the situation. By doing a replay of that situation, and if your emotion was now a more authentic message, and you responded to that authentic message, how could it maybe have turned out better? What would the outcome have been then? How could it have been better for you and the others in the situation?

The balance between feeling good and feeling bad is one indicator you can use to assess to what extent you are a "happy camper" in your own life. The ratio between positive and negative emotions is also an indicator of "the kind of world" you live in. Of course, this "kind of world" is based on how you judge the world and what you pay attention to in the world. If this exercise leaves you with some discomfort, or a concern about the types of messages and emotions you are permitting yourself, then please go back to chapter 2 and look at the options you can explore to change the ratio between feeling good and negative emotions.

Keep in mind also that, at times, negative emotions can be very appropriate. Even though you do not necessarily feel good when you are experiencing negative emotions (and you should do some serious homework if negative emotions make you feel good), there are certain situations and scenarios where, at the very least, the experience and awareness of them are highly appropriate.

The Balance
Some concluding thoughts about creating balance between your positive and negative emotional experiences:
- There are interesting attributes that stand out about positive and negative emotions. These different attributes give positive emotions "bad press", and create a lack of trust in them. When comparing positive emotions with negative ones, it appears that in general positive emotions are softer, or not as intense as negative emotions. Negative emotions, due to their intensity and even pervasiveness, seem to be more "in your face", producing a constant awareness of it.
  Possibly two of the best examples of the power of positive emotions are feeling sexy and being in love. These two emotions are quite compelling when they operate your mind and body. They also appear to be more pervasive for their duration. When you are in love, the entire world is different, and becomes a lovely place to be in. You discover capabilities for writing and creating and saying that you are amazed at. Where did it hide until now?
  However, aside from these examples, negative emotions are seemingly generally better attention-grabbers than positive emotions.
- Negative emotions are not more valid or "better", but appear to have more validity simply due to their compelling nature. Sadly, it appears to be a

universal human phenomenon that people trust bad news much more than they trust good news. In general, people become convinced of bad news more quickly than do they of good news. Not only is the speed characteristic, but it acts like a thought virus: it wipes out all the evidence to the contrary. An example is how one mistake can destroy a relationship or can come to define your expectations of the future or what you feel you deserve. This has two very important implications for getting and maintaining the right balance between positive and negative messages: Despite bad news being such an excellent attention-grabber, one must deliberately seek out the good news and positive judgement. It is there, but you need to see it actively and deliberately; grab it, hold on to it. By becoming aware of how easy it is to slide into bad judgement, you can halt the process for a moment and review the judgement you would be inclined to make (refer to any one of the two chapters on emotional change that would help you reconsider).

- The downside for bad news junkies is that this kind of judgement (or prejudgement) captures you, reduces your range of options, and limits how you can use your capabilities to deal with new situations. As we said before, an emotion is like a magnet: it draws content to itself that is like itself.
Fear, for example, does not leave one with many options except the typical fight or flight responses. In a moment of fear, you do not consider a variety of options or take a step back to reconsider. Fear overpowers and limits you – even in cases where you should know better or have been trained to deal with such events. But the same can be said of sadness, worry, or any of the other negative emotions. It is said that important lessons are learned during bad times.

- This kind of learning happens when you have the ability to stand aside, re-look the situation and ask new questions. In this manner even seemingly life-shattering events can be reinterpreted. If you have not read the chapter on trauma, now is an appropriate time to do so and notice how, in a safe and painless manner, one can re-code and re-judge even a severely painful experience. The key is in the questions you ask and the judgements you are reviewing, both about the event and about the hurt.

- Personal power flows from positive emotions. There is a great deal of research on how positive emotions help us to think better (consider more options), to be more resourceful in approaching solutions to problems, to be healthier, with stronger immune systems, and so on. Not only do we feel better, but we do better: we are more confident of our abilities, more creative, more capable in dealing with bad news, more energized on a behavioural level, and more resistant to tiredness or giving up. We are also more resilient. Feeling good about ourselves, about our situations, about the people around us, seems to make new thinking and feeling possibilities or resources, available to us. Positive feelings give us more resources, which allow us to deal with situations that are not good in much better ways. We are more capable of thinking of more options, alternatives or correctly defining the event without losing hope. "It is bad only because of this event or situation. Despite that, I have in me what it takes to get through this."

In conclusion: The inability to achieve an optimum balance between positive and negative emotions could lead to despondency, sadness and depression. The absence of positive emotions gives you whole life a negative flavour and is a very one-sided view. Talk to anybody who comes from a base of depression, or loneliness, or has suicidal thoughts, and you will hear how lopsided their experience of life is. Life loses its colour; it becomes tasteless. Their lives seem like leftovers that have been forgotten in the fridge. It is as if they are singing the wrong lyrics to the wrong tune. However, when you consider the messages that come from awe, gratitude, love, appreciation, amazement, hope and curiosity, it becomes very clear that life cannot be lived responsibly and fairly without those life-affirming experiences.

CONCLUSION

In the introduction, we started out saying that emotions are such a vital part of human life that it can be said that people live and die for their emotions. In our exploration of this topic, we have seen how, if unbalanced, emotion can be the source of misjudgement, misery and even destruction. They do, however, provide the energy for and is a vital signal of human aliveness.

This book can't possibly say enough about your personal emotions, but hopefully provide you with a tried-and-tested way of thinking about your emotions and enrich the emotional aspects of your experiences. Emotions are signals to be respected since they come from your own wonderful brain and from a level where the speed and function of the mind boggles.

Emotions are messages about how you define the world you live in. This is why the balance between positive and negative emotions are so important. As long as your experience of the world is that it does not meet your standards or criteria, you are very vulnerable. Being a good news junkie, I opt to believe that the balance in life is in favour of the good news. The good news may not be presented to us at the same frequency, nor magnitude, as the bad news, but the preciousness of the good, excellent and beautiful is waiting to be discovered. Reputable researchers insist that one should — and it is possible — achieve an optimal amount of good feelings compared to not so good ones. This is a clear statement of how to be in the world. Some of the stuff that happens to us is impersonal and damaging. What we do with it in our heads and hearts will define the meaning these incidents carry.
My wish is that you may be alive in the best way you know how!!

Further Reading

Andreas, Connirae and Tamara Andreas: *Core Transformation – Reaching the Wellspring Within.* Boulder, Colorado: Real People Press, 1993. (Available on Amazon or through NLP Comprehensive, at AndreasNLPTrainings.com.) It is a "must" part of her program on "the Wholeness Process" (for more information please go to www.AndreasNLPTrainings.com).

Andreas, Steve and Connirae Andreas. *Heart of the Mind.* Boulder, Colorado: Real People Press, 1989. (Available at www.AndreasNLPTrainings.com and on Amazon). Although this book is not specifically about emotions, the NLP way of working with emotions is addressed in many of the chapters.

Cameron-Bandler, Leslie and Michael Lebeau: *The Emotional Hostage: Rescuing Your Emotional Life.* San Rafael, California: FuturePace, 1986. (Available at Amazon.com, or through NLP Comprehensive.) This is still my most favourite book.
Cameron-Bandler, Leslie, David Gordon and Michael Lebeau: *The Emprint Method: A Guide to Reproducing Competence.* Boulder, Colorado: Real People Press. 1985. (Available at Amazon or through NLP Comprehensive.) This book provides an excellent approach to eliciting values and its effect on shaping experience as well as the role of one's time frame in thinking.

Cheal, Joe, has two published articles that are well worth a thorough read-through:
The Landscape of Experience [http://www.gwiznlp.com/wp-content/uploads/2014/08/The-Landscape-of-Experience.pdf] A new NLP model drawing from Emotional Psychology that helps you to identify and understand your own emotional, physiological and cognitive states. The article was originally published in Acuity: The NLP Journal Vol.2 (2011)

The Role of Moods in NLP [http://www.gwiznlp.com/wp-content/uploads/2014/08/The-Role-of-Moods-in-NLP.pdf] What is a mood? Is it different from a state? How could we possibly enhance our moods? The article was first published in Acuity, The NLP Journal Vol.1, No.1 (2010).

Dilts, Robert. To read at least one overview about his writing on neurological levels of experience go to http://www.nlpu.com/Articles/LevelsSummary.htm. A more user-friendly introduction can be read in *NLP For Dummies* by Kate Burton. Robert's more recent work using the neurological levels as a model to understand outstanding entrepreneurs is also worth looking at.

Hall, L. Michael. *Dragon Slaying: Dragons To Princes.* Clifton, Colorado: Neuro-Semantics Publications, 2nd revised edition, 2000. Hall is a prolific writer and the founder of Neuro-semantics. This particular book is an eye-opener regarding the managing of emotions, and a "must" read. Enjoy his other writings at www.neurosemantics.com. Some of his other books that you might find useful include *Games for Mastering Fear: How to Play the Game of Life with a Calm Confidence*, *Games Great Lovers Play: Mastering the Game of Love*, and *Patterns for Renewing the Mind: Christian Communicating and Counseling using NLP and Neuro-Semantics*. Also see *Unleashed!* [2007, chapter 11: Transforming Emotions], *Coaching Conversations* [2011, chapter 7], and *Group and Team Coaching* [2013, chapter 12: Group Emotionsm which deals with emotional intelligence, pseudo-emotions, etc.].

Bodenhamer, Bobby and Michael Hall: *Sourcebook of Magic Volume I* on dealing with emotional patterns. Ch 6: Emotional States.

About the Author

Armand Kruger is a South African clinical psychologist. He obtained a master's degree in psychology, completed the required hospital year internship and qualified through the University of Pretoria in 1972.

After being in private practice for many years, he started to shift his focus to the business world. His passion was to understand peak performers and to find out how they are different from the rest of us. He has done many projects, called modelling, to describe the thinking and behavioural processes of peak performers in a range of industries in South Africa, Europe, England and the USA. Some of these are listed on his web page at www.peakperformer.co.za.

Even though he has written a good number of articles and blogs, this is his first book. You can read more of his articles on his website or write to him at armand@peakperformer.co.za if you have specific enquiries.

Acknowledgements

Looking back over time, I have to say that I was standing on the shoulders of giants when I wrote this book. I would like to mention them in the order that they appeared in my life:

Steve and Connirae Andreas: You confirmed that my connection in NLP was a good one.

Ed and Maryann Reese: The advanced training you gave me really made me see NLP in action.

John Grinder: You taught me to hear and see patterns of excellence and beauty (called modelling). I still hear your voice.

Leslie Cameron-Bandler: The time I spent with you and Michael was an amazing opportunity to learn and share.

Michael Hall: The thinking and methodology of meta-states was a big "wow"-moment in my personal development.

Robert Dilts: Though we have had a few opportunities to meet, it is your writing that has provided constant spiritual companionship to me on my journey.
I mention these names, and virtually no reference to NLP, or to the above names in my book, except Leslie. How come? This is not an NLP book. This is a book about emotions. Based on, and written for, self-discovery. It was initially written when the field was wide open and Daniel Goleman risked writing about it through his concept of "emotional intelligence." This book, however, provides another kind of intelligence about emotions.

Almyne, a friend and thought-partner: Thank you for your constant support in bringing this book to life.

Etsko, Esma: You salvaged a book that I nearly gave up on.

Izelle: when the thank you's stop